A DEFENCE AND CLARIFICATION OF THE
TARIQA TIJANIYYA AND THE TIJANIS

First published in 2015 by

Fayda Books
1677 Dorsey Avenue
East Point Georgia 30344

http://www.faydabooks.com
orders@faydabooks.com

© Copyright Fayda Books 2015

ISBN 978-1-7339631-8-3

No part of this book may be reproduced in any form without prior permission of the publishers. All rights reserved.

Printed and bound in the United States

A Defense and Clarification of the Tariqa Tijaniyya and the Tijanis

Shaykh Al-Islam Al-Hajj
Ibrahim Niasse al-Tijani al-Kaolacki

Translated by

MUHAMMAD HASSIEM ABDULLAHI
AL-TIJANI AL-IBRAHIMI

Contents

Publishers Preface	9
Translator's Introduction	11

A DEFENSE AND CLARIFICATION OF THE TARIQA TIJANIYYA AND THE TIJANIS — 33

Preamble	35
CHAPTER ONE *Definition of the Tariqa Tijaniyya*	37
Text of Sidi Ibrahim ar-Rayyahi Defining the Tariqa Tijaniyya	38
Among the Conditions of Tariqa Tijaniyya is Observing the Religious Obligations	42
The Tijani Disciple and al-Qur'an	42
The Tijani Disciple and Occupying one's Time with Dhikrullah	43
The Shari'a is the Criterion and Balance (*Mizan*) of the Tijani	43

The Tijaniyya is a Tariqa of Knowledge	44
The Tijaniyya is a Tariqa of Jihad in the Cause of Allah	45

CHAPTER TWO — 47
Lies and Fabrications Against Shaykh al-Tijani ؓ and Attempts to Alter the Book Jawahir al-Ma'ani

CHAPTER THREE — 51
Seal of the Saints —Description of the Seal of the Saints by Hakim al-Tirmidhi

Praises from the 'Ulama and the Shuyukh Concerning Shaykh al-Tijani	54
Some of the Praises of Moroccan Scholars for Shaykh al-Tijani ؓ	54
Praises from Tunisian Scholars for Shaykh al-Tijani ؓ	57
Praises from Scholars from al-Sham for Shaykh al-Tijani ؓ	57
Praises of the Scholars from Egypt for Shaykh al-Tijani ؓ	58

CHAPTER FOUR — 61
Tijani Scholars

Some of the Tijani Scholars in Morocco and Senegal	62

CHAPTER FIVE — 63
Refutations of Tijaniyya

The Refutation of the Tijanis is a Deliberate Injustice	63
Refutation & Negative Criticism is According to Comprehension	64
Attachment of the Tijanis to the Qur'an and Sunna	65

The Tijanis are among those who Remember Allah Much	66
The Tijanis are Malamatiyya (The People Of Blame)	66
The Wird of the Tijaniyya is not an Innovation	68
The Litanies (*Awrad*) of Tijaniyya are the Litanies of Prophet Muhammad	69
The Dhikr of the Tijaniyya is the Sunna of the Prophet Muhammad ﷺ	70
The Weight of La Ilaha Ill Allah in the Scale	70
The Recompense of the Tahlil is a Favor of Allah	71
La Ilaha Il Allah is the Best Deed	73
Whoever Bears Witness to La Ilaha Il Allah Enters the Paradise	73
Bearing Witness to La Ilaha Il Allah is an Expiation	74
La Ilaha Il Allah Erases the Sins	74
La Ilaha Il Allah is Salvation for he who Bears Witness	75
False Swearing La Ilaha Il Allah Requires Expiation	75
La Ilaha Il Allah is Safety for the one who Says it	76
La Ilaha Il Allah is a Treasure	76
La Ilaha Il Allah on the Ear of a Fish	77
La Ilaha Il Allah on the Pillar of al-Jannat	78
Verses of Poetry Concerning the Tariqa Tijaniyya and its Litanies	79
From the Qasida of Amir al-mu'mineen Muhammad Bello (d.1837) in Praise of Shaykh Ahmad al-Tijani	81

CHAPTER SIX   85
Praise for the Book al-Bayan wa'l-Tabyin

APPENDIX *Tijani Scholars*	87
Who is Shaykh Ibrahim ﷺ?	89
His Birth ﷺ	91
His Upbringing ﷺ	91
His Teaching His Students the Sciences ﷺ	92
His Entering the Tariqa ﷺ	92
His Ascendancy to the Peak and Summit of the Sciences ﷺ	94
His Excellent And Glorious Qualities ﷺ	94
The Excellence of his Poetry and Prose ﷺ	95
His Writings ﷺ	95
The Description of his Good Morals and Character ﷺ	102
His Generosity and Liberality ﷺ	104
His Move to a New Village and his Building the Zawiya of Ahl Dhikr	104
His Relation to his Father ﷺ	105
His Relation to his Mother ﷺ	106
Her Virtues, Deeds and Morals ﷺ	108
ENDNOTES	111

Publisher's Preface

This short book exists in order to present to the Muslim as well as the non-Muslim english speaking public, a simple yet concise explanation of the Tariqa Tijaniyya. It was written by Shaykh al-Islam al-Hajj Ibrahim Niasse, as a defence of the Tijani Sufi Path and its adherents.

It is with great pride and excitement that we were able to publish and present the English translation of this critically important work to the world.

Anyone that reads it with the eye of fairness will be forced to surrender to the proofs and truths that the Shaykh brings forth.

May Allah bless our guides, may He benefit us by them and may we draw closer to Allah and His Beloved Messenger. Amin

Ibrahim Ahmed Dimson
PUBLISHER, FAYDA BOOKS

In the Name of Allah, Boundlessly Gracious, the Merciful

اللّٰهُمَّ صل على سيدنا محمد الفاتحم لم أغلق والخاتم
لم سبق ناصر الحق بالحق والهادي إلى صراطك
المستقيم وعلى آله حق قدره ومقداره العظيم

Translator's Introduction

This book, written by Shaykh al-Islam Al-Hajj Ibrahim "*Baye*" Niasse ﷺ (d.1975) is a concise and lucid clarification of the Tariqa, or Sufi order of Shaykh Ahmad ibn Muhammad al-Tijani ﷺ (d.1815). The Tariqa Tijaniyya is a Spiritual Path which is based entirely upon the Glorious Qur'an and the Sunnah (traditions) of Prophet Muhammad ﷺ. It is therefore a Muhammadan Path *(Tariqa Muhammadiyya)*, whose adherents have extinguished themselves in the love for their illustrious exemplar, while holding firm to his ways. *"Indeed in the Messenger of Allah you have a good example to follow—for him who hopes for (the Meeting with) Allah and the Last Day, and remembers Allah much."* (33:21). The followers of the Tijani path are devoted to emulating his noble characteristics, in both word and deed, as his character has been described as *"the Qur'an walking"* and his sole mission was the beautification of character traits.[1] So, within the boundaries of these two things is found the Tariqa and *"outside of the Qur'an and the Sunnah there is nothing called the Tijaniyya."*[2] The founder of the Tariqa

A DEFENSE AND CLARIFICATION OF THE TARIQA TIJANIYYA AND THE TIJANIS

has clearly expressed this in his well-known words: *"If you hear anything attributed to me, weigh it on the scale of the Sacred Law (Shari'a). Whatever is in conformity with it, take it; whatever contradicts it, leave it."*

The essence of the Tariqa Tijaniyya is the spiritual reality of Prophet Muhammad ﷺ, or *Haqiqatul Muhammadiyya*, which means his existence as a Messenger to the entire Universe of men, jinn and all existing things and has a message that extends beyond space and time. *"And We have only sent you (Muhammad) as a mercy for the 'Alamin (mankind, jinn and all that exists)."* (21:107). The Prophetic Truth is omnipresent, evident and able to be seen in all things, for it is the honorable spirit *(ruh)* of the Prophets, which Allah has created first of all.[3] In recent years there has been an attempt made by some to disconnect *Tasawwuf*, or Sufism, along with its esoteric knowledge and elucidation, from the Islamic tradition itself—leaving only a shell and a form of the broad and comprehensive *Deen* of Islam. It is like removing the spirit from the body! This novel and new-fangled conception of Islam has caused one writer to observe: *"In these days, when the image of Islam provided by modernist and fundamentalist Muslims seems so superficial and uninspiring, it is good to hear from great traditional authorities..."* [4] The reason for this lack of inspiration in this distortion of Islam is precisely because it does not consider the spiritual essence *(ruh)* of the human being and only busies itself with issues of controversy and scandal, while ignoring the great traditional (classical) authorities of Islam, as well as the contemporary ones. Allah says in the Qur'an, *"They know only the outside appearance of the life of this world and they are heedless of the Hereafter. Do they not think deeply (in their own selves) about themselves...?"* (30:7-8) and *"They ask you about the Ruh (spirit). Say: the spirit is from the order of my Lord and you have been given very little knowledge of it."* (17:85).

According to Shaykh Ahmad Zarruq ﷺ (d.1493), *"Sufism has been defined, described and explained in approximately two thousand ways, all of them related to the importance of genuine dedication to Allah, and each perspective represents an aspect of it, but Allah knows best."*⁵ Imam al-Junaid ﷺ (d.910) has been quoted as saying, *"It means that The Real makes you die to yourself and live for Him."* and *"It means that you exist for the sake of Allah without any other attachment."*⁶ When asked about the reality of Sufism, Sidi Abu Hamza al-Baghdadi ﷺ said, *"It is imitation of the Messenger of Allah ﷺ. There is no guide on the path to the Lord except in following the Beloved Messenger. Whoever makes his soul adhere to the courtesies of the Sunna, Allah will illuminate his heart with the light of direct experiential knowledge of Allah (ma'rifa). Indeed, there is no spiritual station more noble than following the Prophet in his commands, deeds, words and character."* According to Shaykh Ahmad Tijani ﷺ, *"Sufism is carrying out the Divine commands and avoiding the prohibitions, externally and internally, with regards to what pleases Him and not what pleases you."* Shaykh al-Islam Ibrahim Niasse ﷺ succinctly expressed the central point of the subject, writing in his luminous book *"Kashif al-Ilbas"* (Removal of the Cloak): *"Sufism is the expression of a knowledge flaring forth from the hearts of the Saints until their hearts have obtained enlightenment through acting on the Qur'an and the Sunna. For all who act in this way will be awakened and ignited knowledge, secrets, and realities impossible for tongues to describe."*

From these few statements we can deduce and conclude that Sufism is not an innovation, or *bid'a*, as some claim, but is clearly established upon the Book of Allah and the Sunna of the Prophets. Sufism is the Islamic Science of self-realization and its objective is the preparation for that which will unite one to perfection. The ultimate aim and purpose of *Tasawwuf*, or Sufism, is the purification of the heart of Muslim men and women, so those who wish may enter the third and final stage or dimension of the *Deen* of Islam—which is the station of spiritual perfection, or *Maqam al-Ihsan*...described by Prophet Muhammad ﷺ in his saying: *"(It implies) that you worship Allah as if you are seeing Him, and if you are not seeing Him, (then perceive) that He is seeing you."* ⁷

The Tariqa Tijaniyya is a shoreless ocean of spiritual jewels and a treasure chest of Divine knowledge that puts Muslims on the path of the Prophets—which is the path of Nearness and Proximity with Allah. Simply put, it is the path of *Ihsan*. Allah says in His Noble Qur'an, *"Who is better in Deen than the one who submits his face to Allah, being a Muhsin?"* (4:125) and *"Verily, Allah loves those who have Ihsan"* (2:195) and *"Allah's mercy is near to those with Ihsan."* (7:56) and *"Verily, Allah is with those who have Ihsan."* (29:69). What more incentive does anyone need to aspire to other than being among those whom Allah is loving and is constantly with? Shaykh Hassan Ali Cisse ﷺ (d. 2008) has given further illumination on the objective of the Spiritual Path when he wrote: *"Tariqa is built upon sincerity in the truthful attention to Allah, by expelling anything else in one's dealing with The Truth. This is not possible for him who secretly delights in his ego-self (nafs), plunging it into lusts and wicked desires. The Sufis are the true servants, they are the ascetics in every age."* ⁸

The Spiritual Path of Shaykh Ahmad Tijani ﷺ is indeed the *"firm handhold that will never break"* (2:256), which leads its members to the Straight Path *(siratul mustaqim)*, as Allah says: *"And whosoever submits his face (self) to Allah, while he is a Muhsin, then he has grasped the most trustworthy handhold."* (31:22). The Tariqa is the gateway to righteousness and fearful awareness or *Taqwa*⁹, and the fear of God is indeed, the beginning of wisdom and the path by which a person is freed from any material or spiritual difficulty. *"And whosoever fears Allah and keeps his duty to Him, He will* *make a way for him to get out (from every difficulty). And He will provide him with sustenance and wealth from sources he never could imagine."* (65:3).

The author of this book demonstrated in both word and deed that the Tariqa Tijaniyya is among the 'orthodox' Sufi schools for the souls purification and refinement, completely adhering to the way of Prophet Muhammad. He said,

> Let the humans and jinn (*al-thaqulan*—the 'two dependents') bear witness that we hold fast to the rope of the Muhammadan Sunna; that we hold fast to the path of the Prophet, the Master of the first and the last (*sayyid'l awwalin wa'l akhirin*). We walk in the light of his teachings, and vie in following his guidance, which is the savior from calamities (*al-'asim min al-qawasim*). The Tariqa is one of the schools of purification (*tazkiyya*), Spiritual training (*tarbiyya*) and refinement of character (*tahdhib*). So praise be to Allah, Who guided me to hold fast to it, to adopt its discipline, draw from its lights, benefit from its blessings, work with its pioneers and men of distinction. Within the Tariqa I live, and within it I will die, and I will be resurrected with my Master, Abu'l Abbas Ahmad ibn Muhammad al-Tijani al-Hasani, may Allah be pleased with him and grant him His pleasure and may He be pleased with us through him. Ameen! This Tariqa Tijaniyya is the Tariqa of the scholars and the righteous (*tariqatul 'ulama wa's sulaha*) it is a school that produces the guardians of the Deen and the Sacred Law (*hama't deen wa's Shari'a*), beginning with Shaykh Tijani himself...[10]

This translation of the Arabic work of "Shaykh al-Islam" al-Hajj Ibrahim Niasse into English is a much needed clarification of the Tariqa Tijaniyya in particular and of Sufism in general. Being the most influential and consummate Muslim scholar and Sufi mystic from the African continent in the 20th century, as well as being the "Owner of the Tijani

A DEFENSE AND CLARIFICATION OF THE
TARIQA TIJANIYYA AND THE TIJANIS

Flood",[11] Shaykh Ibrahim ibn Al-Hajj Abdullahi Niasse ؓ is more than qualified to make such a defense and clarification of the principles of this noble Tariqa, and we are obliged to learn from such an authority! *"So ask the people of Dhikr if you do not know."* (16:43/21:7)… *"These things are given to us and to the people through the Grace of Allah, but most of the people are not grateful."* (12:38). We include in this preface a brief overview of the life of the founder of the Tariqa taken from texts such as *"Jawahir al-Ma'ani"* by Sidi Ali Harazim, *"Al-Fath ar-Rabbani"* by Shaykh Muhammad ibn Hasanayn at-Tafsawi, *"Futuhat ar-Rabbaniyya"* by Shaykh Ahmad Shinqiti, *"Bughyat al-Mustafid"* by Shaykh al-Arabi ibn as-Sa'ih, *"Khashif al-Hijab"* by Shaykh Ahmad Sukayrij, and *"The Path of the Prophet: Shaykh Ahmad Tijani and the Tariqa Muhammadiyya"* by Sidi Zachary Valentine Wright.

Shaykh Sidi Abu'l Abbas Ahmad ibn Muhammad al-Tijani ؓ was born on the 12th of *Safar* in the year 1150 AH[12]/1737 in the blessed town of 'Ain Madi in the Southwestern Sahara, a Moroccan territory which is today under Algerian control. He was a descendant of Prophet Muhammad through Fatima az-Zahra's first son, al-Hasan ibn Ali ibn Abi Talib ؓ. His father was Sidi Muhammad ibn al-Mukhtar ibn Ahmad ibn Muhammad ibn Salim ؓ and his mother was Sayyidah A'isha bint Muhammad ibn Sanusi ؓ, both of whom were perfect models of erudition, righteousness and piety. Three generations before the birth of Shaykh Tijani, his grandfather Sidi Muhammad ibn Salim, a righteous saint from the town of Asfi, Morocco, who used to engage in spiritual retreat *(khalwa)* so much, he would have to walk to the Masjid for prayer with his face covered, otherwise onlookers would fall helplessly in love with him and be unable to separate from him due to his lofty station in *Wilaya*[13], moved to 'Ain Madi and settled among the clan of "Tijana". He married into them and thus got the nickname of *"Tijani"*, a surname that permanently passed on to his descendants.

Shaykh Tijani ﷺ became an orphan at the age of 16, with both his mother and father dying on the same day to a devastating plague. The Shaykh was the only surviving member of his family [14] and although this was a tremendously difficult time, he continued to apply himself to his religious studies arduously. Having memorized the entire Qur'an at the early age of 7, according to its own interpretation *(bi tafsirihi)*. He then studied the fundamentals of the Islamic Jurisprudence *(usul fiqh)* of Imam Malik ibn Anas ﷺ from texts like the *"Risala"* of Shaykh Khalil; the *"Mukhtasar"* of Abdur-Rahman al-Akhdari (d.953AH/1538); the *"Risala"* of al-Qushayri (d.467AH/1052); in Logic *(mantiq)* the *"Muqaddama"* of Ibn Rushd (Averroes); he studied the *"Mudawwana"* of Sahnun (Abdul-Salam ibn Sa'id Qayrawani, d.240AH/854) with local scholars, such as Sidi Muhammad ibn Hammu al-Tijani (who was widely praised for his deep knowledge of Qur'an and his visionary experience of the Prophet), Sidi Isa Bouakkaz al-Madawi al-Tijani, and Sidi Mabruk ibn Bu'afiyya al-Madawi al-Tijani. He also studied the Prophetic traditions *(hadith)*, Qur'anic recitation *(tajwid)*, Arabic grammar *(nahw)*, and literature *(adab)*, along with the other branches of traditional Islamic sciences, all of which he mastered. Shaykh Tijani ﷺ described his firm resolve in the path of knowledge by saying, *"When I begin something, I never turn from it."* The Shaykh had been blessed with such great intellectual aptitude and photographic memory, that nothing escaped his comprehension. It has been reported that by the age of 20 he was already a great scholar, jurist and man of letters, such that people were coming to him to partake of his knowledge. (Wright, 2005)

In 1171 AH/1758, at the age of 21, during the reign of the righteous Sultan, Mawlay Muhammad ibn Abdullah (d.1204AH/1789) who ruled Morocco from 1757 to 1789, Shaykh Tijani traveled from 'Ain Madi and entered the famous Al-Qarawiyyin University in Fez to obtain all degrees in the Prophetic traditions *(al-hadith nabawi sharif)*, such as those collected by Imam al-Bukhari and Imam Muslim. Fez had been the long-established spiritual, intellectual, cultural and political capital of the *Maghrib* founded by the righteous descendant of the Prophet, Sharif Mawlay Idriss II ﷺ (d.213AH/798).

While in Fez Shaykh Tijani busied himself with study and with meeting the city's famous scholars and Sufi masters and submerging himself in their science...that of the soul's purification *(tazkiyya't nufus)*. Though he had already, by this time, become a Mufti (a scholar licensed to issue legal decisions), he now directed his zeal and determination *(himma)*[15] to investigating the Divine mysteries and discovering the spiritual realities. This marked the beginning of his inclination towards the Sufi path. He first met the head of the Tariqa *Shadhiliyya-Wazzaniyya*, Shaykh Sidi at-Tayyib ibn Muhammad al-Sharif of Wazzan ﷺ (d.1181AH/1767), who gave him permission to give spiritual instruction *(tarbiyya)* only to have Shaykh Tijani refuse in order to work harder on himself before becoming a spiritual guide. He also met Sidi Abdullah ibn al-Arabi ibn Ahmad ibn Abdullah Mada'u al-Andulusi ﷺ (d.1188AH/1778), who told him that Allah was guiding him *"by the Hand."*

Shaykh Tijani was also initiated into the Tariqa *Qadiriyya*[16] while in Fez by Sidi Ahmad al-Yemeni. He then took the Tariqa *Nasiriyya* (named after Sidi Muhammad ibn Nasir Dar'i ﷺ (d.1085AH/1694) from Sidi Muhammad ibn Abdullah al-Tazzani. He then entered the Tariqa *Ghumariyya* (named after Sidi Ahmad ibn Abdul-Mu'min Ghumari al-Hasani, d.1262AH/1847), first from a *muqaddam*, and then from its founder in a dream. He also took from the saint of Traza, Shaykh Sidi Abu'l Abbas Ahmad al-Habib Tawwash al-Sijilmasy ﷺ (d.1206AH/1791), who predicted an exalted spiritual attainment was in store for Shaykh Tijani and counseled him to increase invocation and remembrance *(dhikr)*.

He likewise met Sidi Muhammad ibn al-Hasan al-Wanjili Zabibi ؓ (d.1185AH/1770), a man well known for his saintliness, who told him at first sight, "*You will attain the station (maqam) similar to that of the great Qutb, Sidi Abu'l Hassan ash-Shadhili*" (d.656AH/1241),[17] and gave the indication that his illumination *(fath)* was to occur in the desert. Shaykh Tijani did not stay in Fez long thereafter and traveled to spend time in another Saharan *Zawiya*, known as "*Sidi al-Shaykh*", where lies the grave and shrine of the famous *Shadhili* Qutb and saint, Sidi Abdul-Qadir ibn Muhammad al-Abyad Smahi ؓ (d.1025AH/1610), and he stayed there in spiritual retreat for 5 years. In the following years Shaykh Tijani traveled back and forth between the desert *Zawiyas* and the towns of the region, like Tlemcen. He busied himself with teaching the interpretation *(tafsir)* of the Qur'an and the Prophetic narrations *(hadith)* in whatever town he stayed in, while continuing his scrupulous discipline of asceticism, which included frequent fasting and supererogatory acts of worship *(nawafil)*.

In 1186AH/1773, at the age of 36, Shaykh Tijani decided to travel to Mecca to perform the major pilgrimage, or *Hajj*. Traveling to the East, he was devoted to meeting the well known Islamic scholars and spiritual masters of the time, just as he had done in the West *(Maghrib)*. In Algiers he met the Sufi master and the *Idrisi Sharif*, Sidi Muhammad ibn Abdur-Rahman al-Azhari ؓ (d.1208AH/1793)—who would later become the eponym of the Tariqa *Rahmaniyya* which has spread widely in Algeria. Shaykh Tijani took the Tariqa *Khalwatiyya* from him and was reinitiated into it when in Cairo, Egypt by the Shaykh Sidi Mahmoud al-Kurdi al-Iraqi al-Misri ؓ (d.1195AH/1780).[18] While in Tunis, he began teaching at the famous Jami'at al-Zaytuna Masjid and University (which predates both al-Azhar in Cairo and al-Qarawiyyin in Fez) and made such an impression there that he was offered a lucrative permanent teaching position by the Emir, Bey Ali (who ruled from 1757-1782). Although the Shaykh refused and continued on his journey to the East, this time spent at Zaytuna (where the Shaykh was well received) no doubt prompted a later rector of Zaytuna, Shaykh al-Islam Ibrahim ar-Rayyahi ؓ (d.1266AH/1850)[19], to pay him homage in Fez and become a major propagator of the Tariqa Tijaniyya in Tunisia (Wright, 2005).

In Egypt, upon first seeing Shaykh Tijani, Sidi Mahmoud al-Kurdi told him, *"You are the beloved of Allah in this world and the next!"* The next day, he asked the traveler, *"What is your desire?"* Shaykh Tijani replied, *"My desire is for the great Polehood (al-Qutbaniyya al-'Adhami)."* Shaykh al-Kurdi informed him, *"For you there is much more than that!"* (laka akthara minha). He gave Shaykh Tijani an *'Ijaza mutlaq*, or unlimited license, to initiate into the Tariqa *Khalwatiyya* and he was given a *Silsila*, or spiritual chain of transmission in this Tariqa. From Egypt, Shaykh Tijani left for Mecca and arrived in the Holy Precincts to perform the ancient rites of the pilgrimage just after Ramadan in 1187AH/1774.

In Mecca, he heard of the saint Sidi Ahmad ibn Abdullah al-Hindi ؓ (d.1187AH/ 1774) [20] —the student of the venerated *Shadhili* master, Sidi Ahmad ibn Muhammad ibn Nasir Dar'i (d.1129AH/1714, who is buried in the Tal'a district of Fez)— so he went to meet him. This mysterious saint from India had not been receiving any guests, as he had made a vow not to speak with anyone except his servant. After persisting with this servant to gain audience and after announcing himself by name, he was granted entrance. Shaykh al-Hindi informed his visitor that *"You are the inheritor of my knowledge, secrets, gifts and lights."* He informed Shaykh Tijani that he himself was to die in a matter of days (and it happened on the exact day he had predicted for himself), but gave instruction that he should go visit the Cardinal Pole of the Age *(Qutb Zaman),* Sidi Muhammad ibn Abdul-Karim as-Samman ؓ (d.1189AH/1775) in Medina, and also gave him glad tidings that he would attain the spiritual station of the *Qutbaniyya* of Sidi Abu'l Hasan ash-Shadhili (d.656AH/1241) just as he had been told by Sidi Muhammad Wanjili of Fez.

In Medina, Shaykh Tijani performed all the rites of visitation *(ziyara)* to the tomb of the Messenger of Allahs, where Allah "*completed his aspiration and longing to greet the Prophet.*"[21] Having been informed of the presence of Shaykh as-Samman, he sought to meet with him. Shaykh Muhammad ibn Abdul-Karriem as-Samman was the guardian of the Prophet's blessed grave and an erudite scholar who authored several Sufi books, one of which is "*al-Futuhat al-Ilahiyya fi'l Tawajjuhat ar-Ruhiyya*" (Divine Openings in the Spiritual Pursuits), where he expounds on the concept of *Haqiqa al-Muhammadiyya* and the method of attaining union with its reality.

It was on account of his founding a new *Tariqa* that Shaykh as-Samman became widely known. He combined the *Qadiriyya, Nasariyya,* and *Naqshabandiyya* orders with the *Khalwatiyya* (through his Shaykh Mustafa al-Bakri ؓ of Egypt, d.1162 AH/1749).[22] This became known as the Tariqa *Sammaniyya*. The two had an intense spiritual connection as Shaykh Tijani ؓ was told of what lay in store for him by Shaykh Muhammad as-Samman. He gave Shaykh Tijani the prediction that he was to realize his highest spiritual aspiration and gave him the glad tidings that he would attain the "Greatest Comprehensive Pole" (*al-Qutbaniyya al-Jami' al-'Udhma*). He was given special license *('ijaza)* in the "Beautiful Names" (*Asma al-Husna*)[23], the "The Prayer of the Sea" (*Hizb al-Bahr*) of Shaykh Abu'l Hassan ash-Shadhili (d.656AH/1241), the "Daily Office" (*Wazifa*) of Shaykh Ahmad Zarruq (d.899AH/1484), the "*Dalail al-Khayrat*" of Shaykh Muhammad ibn SulaIman al-Jazuli; and the "*al-Durr al-'Ala*" of Shaykh Muhyideen ibn al-'Arabi al-Hatimi (d.636AH/1221).

A DEFENSE AND CLARIFICATION OF THE TARIQA TIJANIYYA AND THE TIJANIS

Leaving from the Holy Precincts *(Haram ash-Sharif)*, Shaykh Tijani then traveled back to Tunis and from there went to Tlemcen and stayed for 3 years. In 1191AH/1779, when the Shaykh was around 42 years old, he made his second trip to Fez from Tlemcen with the intention of visiting the shrine of the founder of the city of Fez, Mawlay Idris II (d.213AH/798). On the way, he met with his first two permanent disciples, Sidi Muhammad ibn al-Mishry al-Hasani[24] ﷺ (d.1224AH/1809) of Takrak (Constantine) and Sidi Ali Harazem al-Barada[25] ﷺ (d.1218AH/1803). Sidi Muhammad al-Mishry had been a *Faqih* (doctor of law) in Algeria, who was also known for his poetry and mysticism. He used to write the replies and answers on Shaykh Tijani's behalf, as well as lead the prayers as Imam for Shaykh Tijani and his followers until 1208AH/1793, the year that Shaykh Tijani started to lead the prayers himself, in compliance with the instruction of his noble ancestor, Prophet Muhammad.

Sidi Ali Harazem, who is called *"Khalifa al-Akbar"*, was also an erudite scholar and consummate mystic. When Shaykh Tijani first met him in Wajda, Eastern Morocco, he told him: *"You have long been notified in dreams that your guide on the Path is a man named Ahmad Tijani."* When Sidi Ali affirmed the words spoken by Shaykh Tijani, the Shaykh said *"I am he."* The Prophet is reported to have told Shaykh Tijani in a vision, *"O Ahmad, consult with your greatest servant (khadimik al-akbar) and your beloved Harazem, for he is for you what Aaron was for Moses."* The two of these close disciples were initiated into the Tariqa *Khalwatiyya* and taught certain spiritual secrets and special knowledge. He told them of his continued need to go on seeking greater illumination and that they should anticipate more.

After visiting the shrine of Mawlay Idriss II, Shaykh Tijani ﷺ went back to Tlemcen and then departed to the Qasr al-Shallala and then to Abu Samghun, a Saharan oasis located south of Geryville, where he settled. A year later, in 1196AH/1784, he announced that the Holy Prophets had authorized him, in a wakeful daylight vision *(yaqazatan)*[26], to establish his own Tariqa...the *Tariqa Ahmadiyya-Muhammadiyya Ibrahimiyya Hanifiyya Tijaniyya*[27]. The Prophet told him that he no longer had need for any of the chains of authority *(silsila)*, which had been the tradition of all the Sufi orders. The Prophet ﷺ had granted him permission to give *"Spiritual training to the creation in both the general and universal."* This was during a period when the Shaykh had fled from contact with people in order to devote himself to his own personal purification and development, and had therefore felt unworthy to consider himself a Shaykh until this permission was granted. He was commanded by the Holy Prophet ﷺ to cease his devotion to all the orders that he was previously affiliated with and informed him that he was to take the path to the knowledge of God (Sufism) directly from the Prophet himself, saying:

> You are not indebted for any favor from the Shaykhs of the Path, for I am myself your medium and means *(wasita)* and your support in the (spiritual) realization, so abandon all that you have taken from all other orders and hold fast to this Tariqa—without seclusion *(khalwa)*, or withdrawing from the people *('uzla)*—until you reach your promised spiritual station *(maqaam)*, and you will attain your state without constriction, difficulty or excessive effort. And leave (or stop seeking from) the assembly of the Saints.[28]

The Prophets had furthermore given him the basis of a new litany *(wird al-lazim)* to transmit without restriction, to any Muslim (male or female) who seeks and desires it and accepts to abide by its conditions.[29] This *wird* consisted of 100 *Istighfar* (to seek Allah's forgiveness), as repentance and the request for Divine forgiveness is the means to become cleansed of any stain of sin; and 100 *Salat 'ala Nabi* (prayers upon the Prophet), by which one merges into the purity and light of the Prophets...the best of which is *"Salatul Fatihi"*. In 1200ᴀʜ/1787, the Prophets completed the *wird al-lazim* by adding 100 *Hailalah*—*"la-ilaha illa'Allah"*, the proclamation of the Oneness of Allah-"There is no god but Allah".

This sacred Tijani *wird* is clearly based on the principles of Qur'an and Sunnah. Allah says, *"...and seek for His forgiveness, for He is always forgiving."* (110:3) and *"...nor would Allah punish them while they seek for His forgiveness."* (8:33) and the Prophet is reported as saying, *"By Allah! I seek Allah's forgiveness and turn to Him in repentance more than seventy times a day."* [30] And in another narration, *"...one hundred times a day."* Allah says in His Book, *"Verily, Allah and His angels are sending blessings on the Prophet. O you who believe, send salutations of peace and blessings upon him."* (33:56) and the Prophet ﷺ has said, *"Whoever offers one Salat (prayer) on me, Allah makes ten for him. When he prays on me ten times, Allah will pray upon him one hundred times When he offers one hundred prayers upon me, Allah will return one thousand prayers to him and if he offers one thousand prayers upon me, he shall rub shoulder to shoulder with me at the gate of paradise."* [31] Allah says, *"So know! There is no god but Allah, and seek forgiveness for your sin, and also for the believing men and believing women ..."* (47:19) and *"O you who believe! Remember Allah with much remembrance."* (33:41) and *"Therefore remember Me, I will remember you. Be grateful to Me and do not reject (faith)..."* (2:152) and *"...and remember Allah much, so that you may be successful."* (62:10). The Prophet said, *"The best declaration of remembrance is the one which I and all the prophets before me recite, it is the Divine phrase 'La ilaha il Allah."* [32] In a *Hadith Qudsi*, Allah says through the Prophet, *"La ilaha il Allah is My fortress, whoever enters My fortress is saved from My punishment."* [33]

Due to the abundant *baraka* contained in this sacred Muhammadan *wird*, the Tariqa Tijaniyya gained wide acceptance immediately after its birth, with Shaykh Tijani becoming so well-known that great masses of people started visiting him to receive his *wird* and to gain a connection with him. After this grand spiritual illumination (*fath al-akbar*), the Shaykh remained in Abu Samghun for about fifteen (15) years. In 1213AH/1798, when the Shaykh was 63 years old, he permanently settled in the blessed city of Fez along with his closet companions, who began to hear *"from him what we had not heard before in regard to the sciences and the secrets."*[34], and this marked the real beginning of his Tariqa. In Fez, he was well received by the Amir al-Mumineen, Sultan Mawlay Sulaiman ؓ (d.1238AH/1823).[35] This is also the year he gave Sidi Ali Harazim ؓ the instruction to begin the compilation of the book *"Jawahir al-Ma'ani wa-Bulugh al-Amani fi Fayd Sidi Abu'l Abbas at-Tijani"* (The Pearls of Meanings and Attainment of Aspirations in the Flood of Sidi Abu'l Abbas Tijani) by an order from his noble ancestors. The Prophet said to him, *"This is my book and I am its author." (Kitab-i huwa wa ana al-ladhi katabtuhu).*

One year after his return to Fez in the sacred month of *Muharram* of 1214AH/1799, Shaykh Tijani ؓ attained the station of "The Great Comprehensive Cardinal Pole" (*maqam al-qutbaniya al-jami' al-'udhma*), which he had ardently sought. One month and a few days later (on the 18th of *Safar*) he was promoted to the spiritual station of "Concealment" (*al-Katmiya*)—being called the "Hidden Cardinal Pole" (*al-Qutb al-Maktum*). Shaykh Tijani declared that the Prophetsappeared to him in daylight (in a wakeful state, not sleeping) and told him that he is in fact the *al-Qutb al-Maktum* and the *Khatm al-Wilayat Muhammadiyya* (Seal of Muhammadan Sainthood).[36] Asking the Prophets about the nature of this station, he told him: *"He is the one whom Almighty Allah has concealed from all, including His angels and His prophets, except me".*

There exists an invisible spiritual hierarchy of Saints according to a hadith narrated on the authority of Ibn Mas'ud ؓ, the Prophet ﷺ said:

Allah has on the earth three hundred (servants) whose hearts are in the state of the heart of Adam; He has forty whose hearts are in the state of the heart of Musa; He has seven whose hearts whose hearts are in the state of the heart of Ibrahim; He has five whose hearts are in the state of the heart of Jibril; He has three whose hearts are in the state of the heart of Mikail; and He has one whose heart is in state of the heart of Israfil. If the one (last mentioned) dies, Allah will replace him with one of the three; If one of the three dies, Allah will replace him with one of the five; If one of the five dies, Allah will replace him with one seven; If one of the seven dies, Allah will replace him with one of the forty; If one of the forty dies, Allah will replace him with one of the three hundred; And if one of the three hundred dies, Allah will replace him with one of common folk. Allah uses them to drive affliction away from this Community. [37]

The one who is mentioned in this Prophetic tradition (as the only one of his kind) is the Cardinal Pole *(Qutb)*, he being the Spiritual Helper *(Ghawth)*, and his position and his rank among the Saints is like the point at the center of a circle, the focal point of the well-being of the Universe.

The holder of this station is widely known in Sufi literature as the *"Khatim al-Awliya"*, or the Seal of the Saints. In his book entitled *"Khatim al-Awliya"*, al-Hakim Tirmidhi ؓ (d. 318 AH/905)[38] informs us the *"Khatim al-Awliya"* is the person *"upon whom the leadership (imama) of the saints is incumbent; who holds in his hand the 'banner of sainthood'; and whose intercession all the saints have need of, just as the Prophets have need of (the intercession of) our Prophet Muhammad."* Al-Hakim Tirmidhi goes on to explain that the authority of the *"Khatim al-Awliya"* even extends to the eschatological realm. On the Day of Resurrection he will come forth as the Proof *(hujja)* of the Saints, just as the Seal of the Prophets, our master Muhammad, will come forth as the Proof of the Prophets. Indeed, Shaykh Tijani told his Companions, *"When Allah assembles His creatures at the place of standing, a herald will proclaim at the top of his voice, so that everyone at the place of standing will hear him: "O people of the final congregation, this is your Imam, from whom you obtained your support!"*

Al-Hakim Tirmidhi ﷺ put forward numerous questions in his book *"Khatim al-Awliya"* pertaining to the spiritual station of the *"Seal of the Saints"*, his thirteenth question was: *"Who is it that is worthy* (of being called) *the 'Seal of the Saints' (khatim al-Wilaya), even as Muhammad (may Allah bless him and keep him) is worthy of the (title) Seal of prophecy (khatm al-nubuwwah)?* Shaykh Muhammad ibn Ali ibn al-Arabi al-Hatimi ﷺ (d.1240), who is known as *"Shaykh al-Akbar"* (the greatest Shaykh), wrote in his monumental and illuminating work entitled *"Al-Futuhat al-Makkiyya"* (The Meccan Revelations) more than five hundred years before the physical birth of Shaykh Tijani ﷺ and some three hundred years after al-Tirmidhi posed his question:

> As for the Seal of Muhammadan Sainthood, it belongs to a man of the Arabs, of the noblest of them in lineage and power, who exists today in our own time. I was introduced to him ('urriftu bi-hi) in the year 595AH (1198), and I saw the distinguishing Sign (al-'alamah) which he has, which The Real has hidden in him, concealed from the eyes of His servants (sci., mankind), but which He revealed to me in the city of Fez, so that I might discern in him the Seal of Sainthood (khatam al-Wilaya), he being the Seal of Absolute Prophecy (khatam al-nubuwah al-mutlaq) about which most people know nothing. Allah has afflicted (the Seal) with the people who refute and censure him (ahl al-inkar alayhi) concerning that which he ascertained from The Real in his innermost heart. But just as God has sealed the Prophethood of (all) Laws (nubuwat al-shara'i) with

A DEFENSE AND CLARIFICATION OF THE TARIQA TIJANIYYA AND THE TIJANIS

Muhammad (may Allah bless him and keep him), so has He sealed the Muhammad 'Seal' the Sainthood which emanates from the Muhammadan Heritage (al-wirth al-Muhammadi)—-as opposed to what derives from the other Prophets. For, indeed, among the Saints are those who inherit from (the Prophets) Abraham, Moses and Jesus (etc.), so that these may well be found to exist after this Muhammadan Seal; but after him there shall be no Saint belonging to the Heart of Muhammad ('ala qalbi Muhammad). This is the meaning of the Seal of Muhammadan Sainthood...but I shall not name him.[39]

For more than forty years, Shaykh Tijani was himself the foremost propagator of the Tariqa. From Fez, he organized the international Sufi order which had spread in the lands of the East and West during his lifetime. During this time he appointed *muqaddam* and *khulafa* (representatives and successors), who were also great scholars of the Shari'a themselves, who established new *Zawiyas* in Morocco and elsewhere. Shaykh Tijani remained in Fez until he transitioned from this life to his eternal abode On High, Thursday, the 17th of the month of Shawwal 1230AH/1815 at the age of eighty years old. After performing his *Subhi* (morning) prayer, he requested a cup of water and took some drinks and then laid down on his right side and this noble and righteous servant returned to his Lord. The great scholar Sidi Abu Abdullah Muhammad ibn Ibrahim Dukkali led his *janaza*, or funeral prayer, at the Qarawiyyin Masjid, and it was attended by numerous eminent scholars, nobles and saints. Shaykh Ahmad Tijani was buried in his sacred *Zawiya*.[40]

Today there are more than 300 million followers of the Tijani Way in the four corners of the world and approximately 100 million of them have their connection through Shaykh al-Islam Ibrahim *"Baye"* Niasse-Owner of the Tijani Flood! Speaking at the *"International Conference of Tijaniyya"* in

Fez, Morocco in 2007 [41], Shaykh Imam Hassan Cisse (may Allah sanctify his secret) fluently articulated the cause for the continued expansion of the Tariqa saying: "On the foundation of the Book of Allah and the Sunna of Prophet Muhammad, this Tariqa has spread to all horizons, for it is a Tariqa of Truth, and the Truth prevails and is not prevailed upon. If you find the Tariqa Tijaniyya actualizing the brotherhood of Islam, its success lies in rending apart the walls of the ego-selves (*nafs*), penetrating into its depths and illuminating its hidden recesses with beneficial Divine Knowledge. In a similar way, this Tariqa has nullified the borders of nations and erased the differences between the servants of Allah. So here we are in this conference hall meeting with representatives from all parts of Africa: west, east, central and north; and here we have Americans from all different areas: New York, Chicago, Memphis, Atlanta, Detroit... and they are one community! What is between them is only love in Allah, and they have freed themselves of worshiping other than Allah—so that by the Oneness of Allah, the veils have been lifted from them and they have been brought to extinction (*fana'*) and substantiation (*baqa'*) in Allah. They have refused to concern themselves with anything other than Allah. These are indeed true, vigorous Sufis, clothed in the Sunna. Their secret thoughts have been made pure and their external selves have remained steadfast on the Book and the Sunna. They have escaped from the frivolities of the ego-self and have become immersed in Truth's baptism..."the baptism of Allah—and who is better than Allah to baptize." (2:138)" [42]

We bring this introduction to a close by seeking the pardon of Allah and the reader for any mistakes that are found herein and with hope for His Boundless Grace, Mercy and Compassion. May Allah accept this humble effort as sincere for His sake and for the benefit of the Muslims and humanity. May He grant abundant reward to all who have assisted in the

A DEFENSE AND CLARIFICATION OF THE TARIQA TIJANIYYA AND THE TIJANIS

publication of this book—whether financially or by personal effort. By His Benevolence, may all those who contribute to this work be guided in the direction approved by Him and may He fully gratify us, including our Shaykhs, parents, and children, by the grace of our Prophet Muhammad, who receives from Allah the sole privilege of distributing His copious blessings among His patient servants, and by the *Baraka* and *Madad* of our spiritual master, Shaykh Ahmad ibn Muhammad al-Tijani ﷺ and of his sublime mysticism, which transcends space and time. Ameen!

نصيحة مني الى اخواني   فلتمسكوا طريق التجاني
طريق محض والفضل الرضوان   اسس بالسنة والفرقان
خير شيوخ الدهر بالإطلاق   إمامنا التجاني ذو أخلاق
برزخ كل عارف وأس   لهم وينبوع وهو شمس
وخير كل الطرق بالإجماع   طريقه ايضا بلا نزاع

An advice from me to my brothers,
   Adhere to the path of Tijaniyya,
A path of pure grace and satisfaction,
   founded and established upon the path of the Prophet and the Qur'an,
The most excellent Shaykh of all time in any respect,
   is our leader al-Tijani—the possessor of great virtues,
The intermediary and foundation of every scholar of Divine Knowledge,
   he is to them the flowing fountain and the Sun,
And the best path (or Sufi order) by consensus,
   is again his Path without any dispute.[43]

SHAYKH AL-ISLAM AL-HAJJ IBRAHIM NIASSE AL-TIJANI AL-KAOLACKI

عليكم بحبل الله للعبد واثقا ⁦ ⁩ فنهج يناوي الذكر نهج شقاء
وإن قلت هل ذا الورد نهج محمد ⁦ ⁩ أقول نعم وردي لنيل صفاء
فما الورد الا الذكر لله وحده ⁦ ⁩ تصلي على المختار خير وراء
فما فيه ذكر الشيخ او ذكر غيره ⁦ ⁩ فوردي لداء العبد عين دواء
رويدكم لا تنكروا عن جهالة ⁦ ⁩ لبغي وعدوان وعين جفاء

You must hold firm to the rope of Allah,
  For a path which deviates from the Remembrance is a path of misery,
And if you should ask me: 'Is this litany (wird) the path of Muhammad?'
  I will say: 'Yes, my wird is for obtaining purity!',
The wird is nothing but the remembrance of Allah and He alone,
  And sending peace and blessing upon the Chosen One—the best of creation,
In it there is no mention of the Shaykh or any other,
  My wird is the source of medicine for the servants sickness and disease,
Tread lightly and slowly so as not to deny or refuse out of ignorance,
  For injustice and enmity are the sources of estrangement.[44]

Muhammad Hassiem Abdullahi al-Tijani
10 RAMADAN 1430 AH
31 AUGUST 2009

A Defense and Clarification of the Tariqa Tijaniyya and the Tijanis

Shaykh Al-Islam al-Hajj
Ibrahim Niasse al-Tijani al-Kaolacki

Translated by

MUHAMMAD HASSIEM ABDULLAHI
AL-TIJANI AL-IBRAHIMI

In the Name of Allah the Compassionate the Merciful

Preamble

All praise is due to Allah, Lord and Sustainer of all the worlds. Then peace and blessings be upon the best of the Messengers (Muhammad ibn Abdullah) and upon his Family and Companions and all those who follow them until the Day of Judgment.

> *Say: 'This is my way. I call to Allah with the knowledge of certainty (obtained by spiritual insight), I and whoever follows me. Glory be to Allah! And I am not of those who ascribe partners to Him!'*
>
> Surah Yusuf 12:108

CHAPTER ONE

Definition of the Tariqa Tijaniyya

The *Tariqa,* or Spiritual Path of Shaykh Ahmad ibn Muhammad al-Tijani  which he gave to his blessed Companions—who have spread it over the entire earth and by which Allah has strengthened the *Deen* of Islam in numerous countries—is simply organized upon three invocations *(adhkar):*

1. *al-Istighfar* - Seeking the pardon and forgiveness of Allah.

2. *Salat 'ala Nabi* - Prayer of peace and blessings upon Prophet Muhammad using any formula.

3. *Kalimat'l Tawhid* - The statement or proclamation of the Oneness of Allah—*"La ilaha illa Allah".*[45]

We have dealt extensively with the subject of *Tariqa* and *Tasawwuf* in more than one work. The reader, if so wills, can consult our book: *"Al-Kashf al-Ilbas 'an Faydat'l Khatm Abu'l Abbas"* (The Removal of the Cloak concerning the Flood of the Seal—Abu'l Abbas). There one will find scientific and comprehensive knowledge on these topics, this by the grace and favor of Allah upon us and mankind.

One of the celebrated men of this Tariqa, *"Shaykh al-Islam"* in the country of Tunisia— our master Ibrahim ibn Abdul-Qadir ar-Rayyahi ؄ (d.1266 AH/1850)[46] has defined the Spiritual Path *(Tariqa)* in short, concise and clear terms. I reproduce his text resulting from an *'ijaza* (a license authorizing transmission of a body of knowledge) which he gave to Shaykh Abu'l Abbas Ahmad ibn Shaykh Sidi at-Tahir al-Tulayqi in 1244 AH. The erudite scholar and Mufti of Tunisia, Shaykh Muhammad al-Fadl ibn 'Aashur (may Allah extend his life) agreed to make us profit and benefit from the same.

TEXT OF SIDI IBRAHIM AR-RAYYAHI DEFINING THE TARIQA TIJANIYYA

Shaykh ar-Rayyahi ؄ says, "All praise is due to Allah, this is the Tariqa of our Shaykh Abu'l Abbas Ahmad al-Tijani ؄. It consists of the *wird al-lazim* (obligatory litany) to be read daily:[47]

1. Isti'adha (a'udhu billahi minash Shaytanir rajim)
   I seek refuge in Allah from the rejected and cursed Satan

2. Basmala (Bismillah Al-Rahman Al-Rahim)
   In the Name of Allah, The Beneficent, The Most Merciful

3. Istighfar (Astaghfirullah)—100 times.
   O Allah, I seek Your forgiveness!

4. Then Salat 'ala Nabi (prayer upon the Prophet Muhammad) by any formula—100 times. "*Salatul Fatihi li maa ughliq*"—(Prayer of the Opener) is best as it contains the greatest rewards. It is as follows:

اللهُمَّ صَلِّ عَلَى سَيِّدِنَا مُحَمَّدٍ الفَاتِحِ لَمَا أُغلِقِ وَالخَاتَمِ لِمَا سَبَقَ نَاصِرِ الحَقِّ بِالحَقِّ وَالهَادِي إِلَى صِرَاطِكَ المُستَقِيمِ وَعَلَى آلِهِ حَقَّ قَدْرِهِ وَمِقدَارِهِ العَظِيمِ

> O Allah, bestow blessing upon our master Muhammad, the Opener of what was closed and locked, the Seal of what had gone before; the Supporter of the Truth with the Truth, and the Guide to Your Straight Path, and also bless his Family — the blessing should be according to his true value and worth, and his degree and status is tremendously great![48]

> *Allahuma salli 'ala sayyiduna Muhammad, al-fatihi li maa ughliq, wa'l khatima li maa sabaq, naasiril haqqi bil haqqi, wa'l haadi ila sirattikal mustaqeem, wa 'ala alihi haqqa qadrihi wa miqdaarihi'l 'atheem.*

5. La ilaha illa Allah — 100 times.
    There is no god but Allah

This you will say after the *Subh* prayer (morning) and again after *Salatul 'Asr* (afternoon)[49] in accordance with Allah, Exalted is He! saying: "*And remember (wadhkur) your Lord within yourself, with humility and with awe, without loudness in voice, in the mornings and in the afternoon, and be not among those who are neglectful and heedless.*"—(Surah Al-A'raf 7:205)

Then you will perform the *Wazifa* (daily office) once in 24 hours. It consists of:

A DEFENSE AND CLARIFICATION OF THE TARIQA TIJANIYYA AND THE TIJANIS

1. To seek forgiveness with the formula:

   Austagfirullah Al-'Azeemul ladhi La ilaha ilaa Huwa'l Hayyul Qayyum

   I seek the forgiveness of Allah, The Almighty, there is no god but He, The Living, The Self-Subsisting Eternal) 30 times.

2. *Salat Al-Fatihi* — 50 times.

3. *La ilaha illa Allah* — 100 times

4. *Jawharatul Kamal* (The Jewel of Perfection) — 12 times.

It is as follows:

اللّٰهُمَّ صل على عين الرحمة الربانية والياقوتية المتحققة الحائطة بمركز الفهوم والمعاني ونور المتكوّن الآدمي، صاحب الحق الرباني البرق الأسطع بموزن أرباح الملائة لكل متعرض من البحور والألوان ونورك الامع الذي ملأت بي كونك الحائطة بأمكنة مكان اللّٰهُمَّ صل وسلّم على عين الحق التي تتجلى منها عروش الحقائق عين المعارف الأقوام صراطك التامّ الأسقم
اللّٰهُمَّ صل وسلّم على طلعة الحق بالحق الكنز الأعظم إفضالك منك إليك إحاطة النور الملطسم صلى الله عليه وعلى آله سلاة تعرّفنا بها إياه

O Allah, send blessings and peace upon the Source and Fountain of Divine Mercy, the Purest and most Immaculate Gem which encompasses the center of understanding and meanings, the Light of all created beings, the Adamic Man, the Possessor of Divine

Truth; the most luminous flash of Lightning guiding the profitable rain-clouds which fill all the rivers and seas that are vessels and receptacles; Your Bright Light with which You have filled Your Universe and which fills and encompasses all the places of existence and habitation.

O Allah, bestow blessing and peace upon the Source of Truth—from which the Streams of the Realities are manifested; the most upright Source of Divine Gnosis; and Your most Complete and Straight Path.

O Allah, send blessings and peace upon the Appearance of the Truth by the Truth; The Greatest Treasure, Your showering of blessing coming from You to yourself, the All-Encompassing Mysterious Light! May Allah bless him and his Family, with a blessing by which You will lead us to knowing him."[50]

Allahuma Salli wa salam 'ala 'ain al-rahmati rabbaniyati wal yaaqutatil muta haqqatil haa'tati bi markaz al-fuhumi wal ma'ani, wa nurul akwan al-mutakawwantil Adami, Sahab al-haqq al-rabbani, al barq as-ta'i bimuzun arbah almaaliati li kulli muta' arridin minal buhuri wa alwaani, wa nurikal laami'al ladhi malaa'ti bihi kawnikul ha'itah bi amkaniti makani, Allahuma Salli wa salam 'ala 'ainul haqqul lati tatajalah minha 'urush al-haqaa'iqa 'ainul ma'arif al-aqwam, siratikat tam al-asqam, Allahuma Salli wa salam 'ala tal'atil haqqi bil haqq, al-kanzil a'zam ifaadatika minka ilaika ihaa titil nur al-multalsam, Sallallahu alaihi wa 'ala alihi Salatan tu'arifuna biha iyaah

AMONG THE CONDITIONS OF TARIQA TIJANIYYA IS OBSERVING THE RELIGIOUS OBLIGATIONS (AL-FARA'ID)

The fundamental conditions of this Tariqa Tijaniyyah is observing the religious obligations *(al-fara'id)* and to bite down upon them with the molar teeth, the chief of which is the five (5) daily prayers *(Salat)*—preceded by purification with water and fulfilling all of its prerequisite pillars, in accordance with the command of Allah: *"...and establish Salat"—(2:43)*. These prayers should be made in congregation *(jama'at)*[51] with those following the *Sunna*, or way of the Prophet, and not with those who make (abominable) innovations, as Allah continues the verse: *"...and bow down with those who bow down (ar-Raki'un—those who submit themselves to Allah with Muhammad)—(2:43)*, and at the prescribed hours, as Allah says: *"Verily, As-Salat is enjoined on the Believers at fixed hours"—(4:103)*, and with humility, as Allah says: *"Successful indeed are the Believers. Those who offer their Salat with humility and full submissiveness"—(23:1-2)*.

THE TIJANI DISCIPLE AND AL-QUR'AN

In addition to the religious obligations, a Tijani *murid*, or disciple must have a very close connection and relationship to the Qur'an by reciting it, learning it, teaching it and gaining its interpretation! If one is a *Hafiz* (one who memorizes the entire Qur'an), he must strive to complete its reading once each week; or if he can, once every 3 days, that being more perfect. The reading of the Qur'an is the best means of drawing near to Allah, as was confirmed by the vision received by Imam Ahmad ibn Hanbal ﷺ. This is also confirmed by the Qur'an and Sunna of the Prophet ﷺ and by consensus of the 'ulama with intelligence and understanding.

Whoever cannot read the entire Qur'an in 3 days or 1 week, the minimum consists in reading 2 *Hizb* every day[52] or whatever one finds easy, even if just some verses.

THE TIJANI DISCIPLE AND OCCUPYING ONE'S TIME WITH DHIKRULLAH

The teaching of the Tariqa strongly instructs the Tijani disciple *(murid)* to submerge themselves at all times in the remembrance *(dhikr)* of Allah, The Most High. [53] The best of remembrances are those which have come in the Wise Reminder *(Dhikrul Hakim*—Al-Qur'an), such as *"al-Baqiyatul Salihat"* (the perpetual righteous deeds)-saying *Subhana Allah", al-HamduLillah", La ilaha illa Allah", Allahu Akbar"*), and the best of them is saying *La ilaha illla Allah wahdahu laa sharika lahu"* (There is no god but Allah, Who is alone and without partner), after every *Salat*. [54]

THE SHARI'A IS THE CRITERION AND BALANCE (*MIZAN*) OF THE TIJANI

In spite of the clearness of this Tariqa and that it is actually the way of the Qur'an and Sunna, some have decided to criticize Sidi al-Hajj Ali al-Harazim ﷺ, author of the book *Jawaahir al-Ma'ani wa Bulugh al-Amaani fi Fayd Sidi*

A DEFENSE AND CLARIFICATION OF THE TARIQA TIJANIYYA AND THE TIJANIS

Abu'l Abbas Al-Tijani (The Jewels of The Meaning and the Attainment of Hopes in the Flood of Sidi Abu'l Abbas Al-Tijani), simply because he articulated the Divine favor and bounty upon this Tariqa and high station of its people. They could not comprehend the extent of these blessings, so they criticized and denied them and continued denying until they began to personally disparage Shaykh Ahmad Tijani ؅ himself, who openly announced to the whole world in his well-known words: *"If you hear anything attributed to me, weigh the statement on the scale of Shari'a. If it conforms to the Shari'a accept it, otherwise reject it."* This is a statement which leaves no space or opportunity for a fault-finder and it extinguishes every critic.

THE TIJANIYYA IS A TARIQA OF KNOWLEDGE

Many consequences arise from this declaration. Most important among them summarizes itself as follows: Shaykh Tijani ؅ obliges his disciples and followers not only to acquire knowledge, but to continue deepening their knowledge, each one according to his capacity. As only one grounded in knowledge can weigh with the scale of the Sacred Law *(Shari'a)* and refer all of his affairs back to Allah and His Messenger ؅. *"...(and) if you differ in anything amongst yourselves, refer it to Allah and His Messenger, if you believe in Allah and in the Last Day. That is better and more suitable for final determination."* (4:59)."

So the Tariqa Tijaniyya is thus founded upon knowledge and wisdom. Whoever follows Shaykh Tijani ؅ and then makes an abominable errant innovation *(bid'a dalala)*, he only harms and oppresses himself! By his historical declaration quoted above, Shaykh Tijani ؅ freed himself from such persons, while strengthening his own spiritual path and itinerary *(suluk)* in accordance to the Muhammadan Sunna, as recognized by all—the (spiritual) elite and the common alike.

THE TIJANIYYA IS A TARIQA OF JIHAD IN THE CAUSE OF ALLAH

In the book *Al-Islam: The Straight Path"* on page 109, it says:

> *In the seventh (7th) century Hijri (the 13th Christian century), Timbuktu was the center of Islamic culture. Five centuries later this expansion reached a new impulse with the establishment of the Sokoto Caliphate (Founded by Shaykh Uthman dan Fodio ﷺ) to which the majority of West Africa was subject, along with the help and assistance of the Sufi brothers from Marrakesh who were Murids of Tariqa Tijaniyya.*

CHAPTER TWO

Lies and Fabrications

LIES AND FABRICATIONS AGAINST SHAYKH AL-TIJANI ؓ AND ATTEMPTS TO ALTER THE BOOK JAWAHIR AL-MA'ANI[55]

I have in my possession a manuscript-copy of the book *Jawaahir al-Ma'ani wa Bulugh al-Amani fi Fayd Sidi Abu'l Abbas Al-Tijani* (The Jewels of the Meanings and the Attainment of Hopes in the Flood of Sidi Abu'l Abbas al-Tijani) in the handwriting of its compiler & author, *al-Khalifah* al-Hajj Ali Harazim Barada ؓ [56], the same that was in the possession of Shaykh *al-Khatm* Ahmad al-Tijani ؓ for sixteen (16) years! According to my Shaykh and father, the Tijani *Khalifah* in Senegal, Al-Hajj Abdullahi ibn Sidi Muhammad Niasse ؓ, on the authority of Sidi al-Bashir ibn Sidi Muhammad al-Habib ibn Shaykh al-Tijani. Sidi al-Bashir being the one who gave the exceptionally well-preserved historical manuscript-copy to my father al-Hajj Abdullahi Niasse ؓ in the year 1329 AH/1911 when they met in Fez, Morocco (May Allah safeguard it along with its inhabitants!)

The most widely published manuscript contains many discrepancies and foreign things not found in the original copy. I realized this after teaching the book many times to groups of advanced Tijani disciples, as well as in the presence of the scholars of the Tariqa in my school. I read my handwritten copy and they followed with the published version. I constantly informed them of these additions found in their books and not found in the original manuscript-copy of the author.

I informed the Tijani *Khalifah* in Egypt, Shaykh Muhammad al-Hafiz, of this discovery. He borrowed the original manuscript from me and met with the Tijani 'ulama, among them the mayor of the city of al-Isma'iliyya, so that they could confirm my report while comparing the published version. The *Khalifah* then requested me to write a statement to notify all, to be diffused upon need. I did as requested.

I am ready to assist and help anyone who would like to research this issue because the original manuscript-copy will remain with me and all praise and thanks belongs to Allah for it! In addition, I have also read the handwritten manuscript-copy written by Shaykh Muhammad al-Hafiz al-Tijani al-'Alawi al-Shinqiti [57] and have found that it agrees with my original manuscript.

In any event, the attempt to insert and/or conceal things in the books of the 'ulama is not new, but well-known to the researchers *(al-baahitheen)*. Sidi Abdul-Wahhab ash-Sha'rani ؓ said in his book, *Lata'if al-Minan"* (The Subtle Blessings) on page 121, Vol.1. while speaking about Shaykh Muhyideen ibn al-'Arabi al-Hatimi ؓ:

> ...Admittedly, they made him say a whole slew of things contrary to the letter of the Sacred Law

(Shari'a) in his book Al-Futuhaat al-Makkiyya" (The Meccan Revelations) and also in his book Al-Fusus al-Hikam" (The Bezels of Wisdom), as confirmed by Shaykh Badr ad-Deen ibn Jamaa'at and others." The reasons for these attempts are many, but we are well and safe, all praise belongs to Allah, with established facts and certain knowledge concerning our blessed Tariqa Tijaniyya-Muhammadiyya! [58]

I recommend the precious and valuable book written by the erudite scholar, the Judge Qadi Shaykh Ahmad Sukayrij entitled *Jinayat al-Muntasab fima Nusib ila Shaykh Tijani bi'l Kadhib"*, which is entirely devoted to the lies and fabrications directed at Shaykh al-Tijani ﷺ. Within the chapters of this book is abundant benefit and utility. It is published in Cairo, Egypt under the auspices of Shaykh Muhammad al-Hafiz al-Misri al-Tijani.

CHAPTER THREE

Seal of the Saints

DESCRIPTION OF THE SEAL OF THE SAINTS BY HAKIM AL-TIRMIDHI[59]

In his book *Khatm al-Awliya"* (Seal of the Saints), Hakim Al-Tirmidhi ؏ (d.279 AH/905), says on page 421:

> I was asked, 'Describe this Mystic Sufi (*al-majdhub*) for us, who holds primacy and leadership (*al-Imama*) over the Saints and the Banner of Sainthood (*liwa' al-Wilaya*) is in his hand and the entirety of the Saints have need of his intercession, just as all the Prophets have need of our Prophet Muhammad (May Allah bless him and give him peace)?' I answered: 'As for his description, it is as I have already informed you.' (Found in earlier pages of the book of al-Tirmidhi, such as his saying "...the Station of Intercession will be set up for him and he will praise and extol his Lord with such praise and commend Him with such adulation that the Friends

of Allah will recognize his superiority over them with regard to the knowledge of God.)"

I was then asked, 'Why does he have precedence over the Saints so that they have need of him?' I answered: 'Because he has received the "Seal of Sainthood" (*khatm al-Wilaya*) and by this 'Seal' he has gained primacy and superiority by possessing the sincerity of Friendship/Sainthood with Allah and has become the Proof of Allah (*hujjat*) over His saints. I have already mentioned in the beginning of the book the reason for this "sealing"—which is that Prophethood (*an-nubuwa*) is given to the Prophets (peace be upon them all) and is not given to the Seal. Because these (previous Prophets) do not (completely) abandon or relinquish the share of the blemish and fault of the ego-self (*nafs*) and its defects, they then accept our Prophet Muhammad who closes and seals 'Prophethood' (*nubuwwa*), in the same way a contract/covenant (*'ahd*) or a letter is written and then "sealed" so that no one can add to it or take away from it! (meaning that anything arriving to any of these saints would bear the mark of this Seal, just as all the Prophets before Muhammad bore the seal of the prophecy of the final Prophet). I have already described his importance and significance in what precedes. In similar fashion, Allah (The Exalted) makes this Saint (the Seal) to follow the Path and Way (*Tariqa*) of Muhammad, by whom Prophethood is "sealed" by Allah. Just as Muhammad ﷺ is the Proof of Allah on the other Prophets, this Saint has become the Proof of Allah over the other Saints." [60]

It is as if Allah, The Most High, says to the hosts of Saints: 'I gave you Wilaya and you did not fail to mix the ego-self (*nafs*) into it and here is one weaker than you (younger than you & more recent), but who achieved perfection of Friendship/Sainthood (*wilaya*) with a total sincerity and did not give the ego-self (*nafs*) any portion in this affair at all!' All of this occurred in the Unseen (*ghaib*), ⁶¹ by the bounty and favor of Allah (The Exalted) towards this servant (*'abd*) when He gave him the 'Seal' (*khatm*), for the delight and consolation of MuhammadSat the Place of Gathering—so that Satan is made to sit in isolation, seclusion and retreat and also the carnal soul or ego-self (*nafs*) does not find the means to seize its share of the Friendship with God and loses any hope and remains screened. Thus, due to him, the Saints will be delighted and consoled on this Day by the favor and grace (*fadl*) which is made to them. When the frights and horrors (of the Day of Judgment) come to them, he (this Seal) will not be affected. Muhammad ﷺ will come with the Seal (*al-khatm*), so they become safe and immune (*amaanan*) against these terrors and frights. Then this Saint will come with his "Seal" bringing safety to them by the veracity of the sincerity of his Sainthood (*sidq al-Wilaya*). Thus the Saints have need of him.'

The Seal (of the Saints) has an extraordinarily amazing importance, status and position! By Allah, the children of Adam (all of humanity in general) are miraculous and a wonder! Their creation is a grand affair (*al-amr 'azim*) when the intellect (fully) knows and comprehends that Allah created Adam with His own Two Hands! When one knows that this plan or project (of human creation) contains a majestic and grand affair and when he knows and understands that He called him "Khalifah"—representative or viceregent! "And when your Lord said to the angels: 'I am going to place in the earth a viceregent…and He taught Adam all the Names…and when We said to the angels: 'Make obeisance to Adam, they did obeisance…" (2:30-34). This is an extraordinary position when it is understood that a representative or viceregent is generally accepted to have (at least) a branch or division (*shu'ba*) of the capacity of the king he represents!⁶²

A DEFENSE AND CLARIFICATION OF THE
TARIQA TIJANIYYA AND THE TIJANIS

PRAISES FROM THE ʿULAMA AND THE SHUYUKH CONCERNING SHAYKH AL-TIJANI

I have already mentioned in my book *Tanbih Al-Adhkiya* (Exhortation and Warning to the Intelligent), a summary of the relationship of the Islamic scholars in North Africa and elsewhere with Shaykh Ahmad Tijani ؓ. I deliver some here without being too longwinded.

The Scholars of this Deen and the respected *Shuyukh*, well-known in all lands, spoke in praise of our Shaykh, the Seal, al-Tijani ؓ. These are Shaykhs who one cannot suspect of lying! This admiration was for his knowledge, sainthood and gnosis *(ʿilm, wilaya, ʿirfan)*.

SOME OF THE PRAISES OF MOROCCAN SCHOLARS FOR SHAYKH AL-TIJANI ؓ

Among the Moroccans who spoke in praise of him is Sidi Hamdun ibn Al-Hajj, whose son wrote in his book *Al-Ashraf"* (The Noble Ones) that his father had praised Shaykh Tijani ؓ for his knowledge of (the Islamic sciences) and Divine gnosis *(ʿilm waʾl maʾrifa)* saying: *"He is one of the Perfected Ones"* and lauded him in a poem *(qasida)* with these words:

I recommend you to the resplendent light-giving Moon,
Abuʾl Abbas, I mean Ahmad al-Tijani,
  The Sun of Nobility, The Cardinal Pole of the circle of guidance,
The Moon of felicity and happiness, The Star of spiritual perfection,

*The Sea of generosity, our elucidator of Divine wisdom,
Like rare gems in a necklace or crown,
The Leader (Imam) who has risen in ascension by righteousness
without lethargy and laziness."*

Among them is Shaykh al-Talib ibn Al-Hajj, who in his commentary of the book *Al-Murshid"* (The Guide), commenting on the verse *"Obligatory on the Messengers is truthfulness..."*, says: *"The Shaykh, The Knower of Allah ('arif billah), my master Ahmad al-Tijani, may Allah make us benefit from his blessing, says..."*

Among them is the erudite Scholar, the Noble Sharif (and historian of the Maghreb), Sidi Ja'far ibn Idris al-Kattani (d.1912), who mentions in his book *al-Shurb al-Muhtadar wal-Sirr al-Muntazir"* (The Present Beverage and the Awaited Secret), the following: *"Among them is the famous Saint, the Qutb without doubt, the Lorldy Spiritual Helper (Ghawth), Abu'l Abbas, Sidi Ahmad al-Tijani."* Then he added: *"His good qualities are numerous and his spiritual states extraordinary and his station in sainthood (Wilaya) is great."*

Among them is his son, the influential scholar (and another great Moroccan scholar and saint), Sidi Muhammad ibn Ja'far al-Fasi al-Madani al-Hasani al-Kattani (d.1925), who said in his historical masterpiece on the saints and scholars of Fez named *Salwat al-Anfas"* (Relief of the Souls), on page 180 Vol.1:

> The Shaykh who reaches union with Allah, the perfect example, the achieved, the perfected, the entrenched Gnostic, the mountain of Sunna and Deen, the Signpost of those with God-consciousness (*mutaqeen*) and rightly-guided (*muhtadeen*), the very intelligent one, the balancer of exoteric and esoteric knowledge (*Shari'a and Haqiqa*)...Sidi Ahmad al-Tijani.

A DEFENSE AND CLARIFICATION OF THE TARIQA TIJANIYYA AND THE TIJANIS

Among them is the scholar Abu Abdullah Sidi Muhammad al-Qadiri who describes the Shaykh as follows in the book *Raf' al-'Itab wal Malam 'aman qala al-amal bi'l da'if ikhtiraan haram"* (Removal of Blame from those who prohibit the practice of actions based on Weak Traditions) on page 53: *"The Gnostic one, my master Ahmad al-Tijani".* Also in his commentary on the poem *"Al-Burda"* of Imam al-Busayri ☙, he says that his father recommended to him to love Shaykh al-Tijani. Moreover, he says: *"He met his Shaykh and the Shaykh of his father Sidi Abu'l Abbas Ahmad Banaani and he testified to him that he loved this Shaykh (Ahmad al-Tijani)."* And these people were the Scholars of Fez!

Among the scholars of the Maghrib is also the famous *'alim*, the celebrated genealogist, Sidi Ahmad al-Nasiri Alawi ☙, who in his book *Al-Istiqsa"* (The Investigation), mentioned on page 138,vol.4: *"Shaykh Abu'l Abbas al-Tijani is full of influential knowledge".* On page 146,vol.4 he says:

> *As for the Saints (awliya) and their prohibiting the visitation (ziyara), in order to avoid any pretext of (delay or mishap on the Path for the murids), but it is explained correctly and thoroughly, so that the prohibition is not vague and unclear, but only for the sake of the disciples and does not contradict the Shari'a, but is in conformity with it. Allah knows best! This is the position of the Shaykh, the Faqih, the Sufi, Abu'l Abbas Ahmad al-Tijani ☙, who prohibited his Companions from making Ziyara[63] to non-Tijani Saints.*

Finally, on page 150:vol.4, the author says: "The Shaykh, The 'alim, The Gnostic ('arif), The Imam, Abu'l Abbas Ahmad al-Tijani, Supreme Guide of the Tariqa Tijaniyya."

PRAISES FROM TUNISIAN SCHOLARS FOR SHAYKH AL-TIJANI 🙵

Among the people of Tunis is the Shaykh Muhammad Bayram al-Khamis al-Tunisi al-Misri (died in Egypt in 1370AH), who, in his book *Safwat'l I'tidar bi Mustawda' al-Amsar"* on page 32, describes the Shaykh as: *"The Qutb, the righteous (as-salih), my master Ahmad al-Tijani 🙵"*. He also mentions a poem by which Shaykh al-Tijani sought help from Allah when he encountered difficulties in the regions of Tunisia.

PRAISES FROM SCHOLARS FROM AL-SHAM FOR SHAYKH AL-TIJANI 🙵

Among the people of Syria is the Imam, Sidi Yusuf an-Nabahani, who describes the Shaykh in his book *Jami' Karamat al-Awliya"* (Collection of the Miracles of the Saints) on page 349,vol.1 as: *"Leader of the Gnostics (Imam al-'Arifin), one of the major Saints drawn near."* In his book *"Sa'adatou al-Darayn"* (Happiness of The Two Worlds), he says: *"Shaykh al-Tijani was one of those who took his Awrad (litanies) and adhkar (remembrances) directly from the Prophet Muhammad 🙵 in a wakeful state."* He describes in this book certain distinctive characteristics of the special prayer of Shaykh al-Tijani called *'Jawharatul Kamal'* (Pearls of Perfection).

Also among them is the celebrated saint, Sayyid Muhammad Fal ibn Muhammad ibn Ahmad al-'Aaqil, who said in a line of poetry: *"...and Ahmad, known as al-Tijani, endowed with knowledge, secrets and gnosis" (wa Ahmad al-ma'ruf bi'l Tijani, dhul 'ilmi wa'l asrari wa'l 'irfani)*

Also among them is Sidi Abdullah ibn Ahmad Dam, recognized for his high position by all his provincial contemporaries, who describes Shaykh al-Tijani and his Tariqa in a poem as follows:

Whoever wants can doubt the madhab (school or way) of al-Tijani,
   as for me I am convinced of his perfection.
Whoever reads the books that they propagated will see truthful words
   all guiding to the Straight Path.
Those who take his litany (wird) will be guided,
   in counting a certain number (of istigfar, Salat 'ala nabi and "hailala"),
Whoever doubts (the truth of what we've said) will not be safe from embarrassment and will be tested one way or another.
Anyone in the Tariqa who comes with something contrary to the Truth (of Qur'an & Sunna)
   is like a son who contradicts and disobeys his father

PRAISES OF THE SCHOLARS FROM EGYPT FOR SHAYKH AL-TIJANI

In his book *Intashar Al-Islam fi'l Qaratu'l Ifriqiya* (The Spread of Islam on the African Continent), Doctor Hasan Ibrahim Hasan, Rector of the University of Asyut, says on page 44:

> Among the Sufi brotherhoods who have been most effective in spreading Islam on the African continent is the Tariqa Tijaniyya, founded by Abu'l Abbas Ahmad ibn Muhammad al-Mukhtar ibn Salim al-Tijani (1737-1815), originating in the village of 'Ain Madi in Algeria. He made several journeys in the Muslim countries (*bilad al- Islamiyya*) like Tlemcen,

Makka, Medinah and Cairo. He was found near the scholars (Shuyukh) of these cities. Thereafter he founded a new Sufi Order. He visited the Saharan desert (al-Sahra) in 1782 and then finally settled in Fez (Morocco) in 1798 and made it the center of his teaching. He passed a great part of his life there organizing and spreading his Tariqa. He called his Companions 'al-Ahbab' (The Beloved) and prohibited them from joining any other Tariqa. One observes them practicing constant Dhikr (remembrance of Allah), reciting the Qur'an, making supplications, offering Salat 'ala Nabi (prayers on the Prophet Muhammad) and performing their Wird (litany) at precise hours in the day.

We mentioned here just some of the Islamic Scholars *('ulama),* those who are not in the Tariqa Tijaniyya, but nevertheless had nothing but praise and honor for Shaykh al-Tijani.

People are not so courteous and polite to the point of praising a man,
  where they do not find traces of his goodness.

CHAPTER FOUR

Tijani Scholars

We will not go into detail on the number and qualities of the Scholars *('ulama)* of this *Deen* who are to be counted among those who submitted themselves to the spiritual guidance of Shaykh al-Tijani ﷺ and follow his Tariqa, yesterday and today. Their number and their existence in all the lands are enough to illustrate the value of the Tariqa, and all praise belongs to Allah!

We are satisfied to quote passages from the book *"Al-Qayyim al-Iman as-Sahih"* (Clarifying the Authentic Faith) by the erudite Scholar, The Qadi of Morocco, Sidi Ahmad Sukayrij ﷺ. On page 60, he strongly defends Shaykh al-Tijani.
some of the tijani scholars in tunis

Were Shaykh Ahmad Tijani ﷺ to have no other follower but Abu Ishaq Ibrahim ar-Rayyahi, it would suffice us as a proof to also follow him. His erudition and his being a practitioner of his knowledge is more visible than a lit fire on top of a mountain. The ar-Rayyahi family are among the traditional and noble people of Tunisia and among them are the *Khulafa* of our Master ﷺ.

Among the families famous for their nobility and love for Shaykh Tijani ﷺ in Tunisia are the blessed children of al-Nayfar, a family of firm knowledge *('ilmul raasikh)*. Also, the blessed children of Bayrum, a family of high nobility *(al-majdi'shaamikh)*.

SOME OF THE TIJANI SCHOLARS IN MOROCCO AND SENEGAL

We mention in particular those in Fez, the families of Kanun; of 'Alawiyyin; of Mawla Abdul-Malik ad-Darir; of Mawla Abdus-Salaam ibn Umar and others, like the family of Bannani, in which one finds Shaykh Ahmad ibn Ahmad Kellaa Bannani; the family of Qabaaj; the family of Abi Hilali; the family of al-Saqaat—people of sainthood and righteousness; the family of Jasus in Rabat—people of honesty and justice, and others besides them which one cannot count.

These families helped to spread the Tariqa in the East and West. Like the family of Al-Hajj Malik Sy in Tivaouane, Senegal and the family of Al-Hajj Abdullahi Niasse in Kaolack, Senegal and numerous others besides these, whom Allah blessed and honored for their sincerity *(tasdiq wal suluk)* in following this Tariqa Tijaniyyah.

CHAPTER FIVE

Refutations of Tijaniyya

THE REFUTATION OF THE TIJANIS IS A DELIBERATE INJUSTICE

Qadi Ahmad Sukayrij writes in *"Al-Iman as-Sahih"* (The Authentic Faith) on page 90-91: *"Each of these (persons of Tariqa) is with a Community that Allah has joined together and ensured safety, so whoever would seek to make error and misguidance (dalaala) in it would only be unsuccessful. The Ummah of Muhammad ﷺ cannot agree on error. So, to thus expel someone from the Deen of Islam, or make takfir (to declare a Muslim a disbeliever) because of a difference in understanding is unfathomable and certainly not the statement of a Believer."*

One cannot help but laugh when one sees or hears someone criticize these celebrated Friends of Allah, by (wrongly) using the saying of Allah, Exalted is He!: *"Today, I have perfected your Deen for you and completed my favor upon* you..."(Surah Al-Ma'ida 5:3) to declare that they (people of Tariqa) took these saints as lords besides Allah. This is a deliberate injustice. These Shaykhs neither made permissible (that which is Divinely) prohibited, nor prohibited (what is Divinely made) permissible, as did the Christian priests, Allah forbid! They did not invent anything new to this *Deen*. No, they are those who are holding to the Rope of Allah and following the Sunna of Muhammad! They did not order except what Allah and His Messenger ordered and they did not prohibit except what Allah and His Messenger prohibited. Allah has granted success and help to whomsoever among His worshippers follows them and obeys their orders to the best of their ability. By this they come to be those *"...men and women who remember Allah much."* (Surah Al-Ahzab 33:35), or rather, they ascend and rise to become those who call to good, and all praise and thanks belongs to Allah!

REFUTATION & NEGATIVE CRITICISM IS ACCORDING TO COMPREHENSION

The rejection and censure of Shaykh al-Tijani and his followers is a mark of boastfulness and ignorance. Al-Kansusi quotes Shaykh ash-Sha'rani in his book *"Al-Jawaahir wa'l Durur"* (The Jewels and The Pearls):

> I heard my master Sidi Ali al-Khawaas say: "People are arranged in categories:
>
> 1. The General/Common people (*'amma*)
> 2. The Jurists (*fuqaha*)
> 3. The Beginning Sufi (*mutasawwafa*)
> 4. The Gnostic Sufi (*Sufiyyatu 'Arifun*)
> 5. The Perfected Sufi (*kamilun*)

6. The Perfecting Sufi (*mukammalun*)
7. The Cardinal Poles/Axis (*aqtab*)

>Each one necessarily criticizes and denies those who are higher in station because of their ignorance and lack of "tasting" of these states. So, the Jurist (Faqih) criticizes the Beginning Sufi disciple. The Beginning Sufi denies the Gnostic Sufi . However, the Gnostic ('Arif billah) does not deny anyone, having traveled and exceeded the states (of the first 3). So this is what we mean by refutation and negative criticism being in accordance to one's comprehension and not based upon the rulings of Shari'a (laa al-inkar man hayth al-ahkam Shari'a).*"64*

ATTACHMENT OF THE TIJANIS TO THE QUR'AN AND SUNNA

Any sincere (and knowledgeable) person knows that Shaykh Ahmad Tijani ﷺ constantly engaged in remembrance *(dhikr)* of Allah during the hours of the night and at the ends of the day, and he ordered his Companions to do the same. If all the ritual actions of a Tijani disciple ie. performing *dhikr*, reading Qur'an, sending blessing and salutation upon the Prophet, contribute to the remission of sins, then the assertion that whoever assiduously follows this Tariqa will see his/her sins erased is not astonishing or surprising—and we have a beautiful opinion of Allah! (*wa dhunu billlahi jameel*) ⁶⁵

This Shaykh (Ahmad Tijani) and his Companions are those who purify themselves with water, have mastery and perfection in the performance of the five (5) daily *Salat*, recite the Qur'an by memory and by the text, pay *Zakat*, give charity, fast, make the pilgrimage to Mecca and perform *Jihad* in the cause of Allah. All this by the guidance of Shaykh

A DEFENSE AND CLARIFICATION OF THE TARIQA TIJANIYYA AND THE TIJANIS

Ahmad Tijani ﷺ - the evanescent and annihilated in the love of Allah, the scholar, the pious, the ascetic, the one completely devoted to Allah. *(al-fani fi mahabbatullah, al-'alim, at-taqi, az-zahid, al-wara' al-mutabitil ila Allah tabtilan).*

THE TIJANIS ARE AMONG THOSE WHO REMEMBER ALLAH MUCH

This response of the Scholar, the Gnostic, the Jurist, Muhammad al-Kansusi, the 'tongue of the Tariqa', written to Sidi Ahmad al-Kunti, should illustrate this fact:

> By Allah, these people (of Tariqa Tijaniyya) are among the best of this Ummah. They, by the praise of Allah, are pure from any stain. And why should it not be thus, since they fast and stand invoking Allah their Lord, morning and evening...seeking His Face! Among them are those who do not know sleep at night, nor enjoy food or drink in the day, except for the Feast days *(al-'ayaad)*, there are among them those who do not recite less than 10,000 Salat 'ala Nabi with "*Salatul Fatihi li maa Ugliq*" during the day and the night. [66]

THE TIJANIS ARE MALAMATIYYA (THE PEOPLE OF BLAME)

Abu Abdullah Muhammad al-Kansusi[67] continues:

> *The Tijanis claim for themselves no special characteristic of distinction or merit and virtue, or (in general) a difference from the rest of humanity. The master of a craft or skill is occupied in it and he who*

has work or employment is engaged in his profession (each one is busy with all types of normal business), although it is they who direct existence (mutasarafin al-kawn) by true and veracious Spiritual and mystical states (ahwal), and not by particularity or natural preparation or capability. Undoubtedly, they are the Malamati Masters, whose leader is Abu Bakr as-Sadiq al-Akbar ☙.⁶⁸

Shaykh Ibn 'Arabi al-Hatimi ☙ wrote in *Futuhat al-Makkiyya* (The Meccan Revelations) in Vol.1 page 181:

> Know, and may Allah assist you, that this chapter deals with those servants of Allah that are called Malamatiyya, that is, the spiritual men who possess the very highest degree of Wilaya.

> There is nothing above them but the degree of Prophethood. Their Maqam is the station called the "Station of Proximity" (maqam al-qurba). Their specific verse in the Qur'an is "houris guarded in pavilions"(55:72), a verse that, with this specific description of women in paradise and its houris tells us about the souls of those Men of Allah that He has chosen for Himself, that He has preserved, that He has enclosed in the tents of Divine jealousy in every corner of the universe such that no gaze can fall upon them and distract them—but no, the gaze of the creatures could not possibly distract them! Allah has enclosed their outer forms in the tents of ordinary actions and customary devotions such that, from the point of view of apparent practices, they devote themselves only to obligatory devotions or to habitual supererogatory worship (nafila).

> They do not make themselves noticeable with miracles. People do not glorify them, they do not point at them because of their piety, in the sense that people commonly understand, even though no evil can be imputed to them. They are those who remain hidden, they are the righteous, the Faithful guardians of the repository in the universe. ⁶⁹

A DEFENSE AND CLARIFICATION OF THE TARIQA TIJANIYYA AND THE TIJANIS

THE WIRD OF THE TIJANIYYA IS NOT AN INNOVATION

The litanies *(awrad)* of this Tariqa are the litanies of Prophet Muhammad. Those who are devoted to them have the confirmation of its utility and benefit. There is nothing more beneficial to the real and true Muslim than to constantly remember Allah and invite people to Islam by word and deed. *"Who is better in speech than one who calls to Allah, works righteousness, and says, 'I am of those who submit in Islam'?"* (41:33) As for us, we do not declare any Muslim a *"kafir"* or an unbeliever. Because to make *"Takfir"* of any person who faces the Ka'ba (in prayer), or is *Ahl al-Qibla*, is an intolerable position. On the other hand, if someone levels the charge (of *kufr*) against us, we declare the same! This position is based on the word of the ProphetSwho said: *"Whosoever calls his brother a kafir, one of the two will be guilty of it."* [70]

Actually, when a (Tijani disciple) sits in front of a teacher and seeks from him instruction as to what remembrance or *dhikr* to say after the five obligatory *Salat* [71], and the Shaykh tells the student "it is such-and-such"; "this number of times"; "to be said in the morning and evening"; "when making *Wudhu* (ablutions)"; "when going to sleep"; "during the *Witr* prayer"; "when performing *Tawaf* (to circumbulate the Ka'ba)", for example, the enquirer or student does not make an innovation *(bid'a)* nor does the teacher!

THE LITANIES (AWRAD) OF TIJANIYYA ARE THE LITANIES OF PROPHET MUHAMMAD

The Scholar Abu Bakr al-Deymani ash-Shinqiti says in a poem:

Is it unbelief (kufr) for a servant to declare sincerely "There is no god but Allah?
  Or to seek forgiveness hoping for remission of sins which he committed?
O mankind, if this is kufr then persist in unbelief,
  for you will certainly have a blessed and happy end!

Even if Satan would have recommended these invocations their performance would not be any less effective nor the obligation to follow removed, because according to the hadith: *"...he told you the truth although he is a liar."*⁷² So what about when it comes by way of a Saint *(Wali)* from among the Friends of Allah? Moreover, if they are the litanies *(Awrad)* of the Prophet ﷺ. With mutual respect and tolerance, people have affiliated themselves with Shaykh Abdul-Qadir al-Jilani ؓ or Shaykh Abu'l Hasan ash-Shadhili ؓ or with Shaykh Ahmad al-Tijani ؓ - all these are the same litanies *(Awrad)* of Prophet Muhammad ﷺ and none other! This remembrance and praise is of Allah and none else!

A DEFENSE AND CLARIFICATION OF THE TARIQA TIJANIYYA AND THE TIJANIS

THE DHIKR OF THE TIJANIYYA IS THE SUNNA OF THE PROPHET MUHAMMAD ﷺ

We bring this book to a close by mentioning some of the invocations *(adhkar)* which contribute to the remission of sins, so that the only one who remains lost and ruined is the one who desires to be lost and ruined, and those who want to be saved and made alive will be made safe and alive!

In his book *Tabaqat Shafiyyatu'l Kubra*, Tajudeen as-Subki relates: "On the authority of Abdullah ibn Qatada on the authority of his father, the Prophet ﷺ said: *"Whoever says 'I testify there is no god but Allah and I testify that Muhammad is the Messenger of Allah' with his tongue and with sincerity of heart, the Fire (jahannum) is prohibited from touching him."* [73]

THE WEIGHT OF LA ILAHA ILL ALLAH IN THE SCALE

As-Subki continues:

> On the authority of Abdullah ibn Umar, the Messenger of Allah ﷺ said: "On the Day of Resurrection, a man from my Ummah will be brought out in front of all of his fellow creatures, and ninety-nine scrolls will list the charges against him, each scroll stretching as far as the eye can see. He will be asked: 'Do you deny any part of this?' The

man will say, 'No, my Lord'. Then Allah, Glorious and Majestic, will say to him: 'Do you have any valid excuse or good deeds?' The man will fearfully say again: 'No, my Lord'. Allah, Glorious and Majestic, will say to him: 'You have a deposit of good deeds recorded here with Us and you will suffer no injustice today!'. He will then receive a small sheet of paper, on which is written the words: "I bear witness there is no god but Allah and I bear witness Muhammad is His servant and Messenger". Allah will say: 'Prepare for your weighing in the balance.' so the man will say: 'O my Lord, what is this sheet of paper in relation to all these scrolls?' Allah will say, 'You will suffer no injustice today!' He (Glorious and Exalted!) will order the scrolls to be placed in a scale of balance and the small sheet of paper on the other. The scrolls will be light in weight and the slip of paper will be heavy, for nothing matches the weight of Allah's Name!"

THE RECOMPENSE OF THE TAHLIL IS A FAVOR OF ALLAH

(Continuing to quote as-Subki):

Recorded by at-Tirmidhi, on the authority of Layth ibn Sa'd, who mentions similar remarks which support them. One understands by the fact that the balance of the scales fell on the side with the piece of paper (with *"La ilaha ila Allah"* on it), that the double *Shahada* erases sins and is not an innovation. So it isn't strange, that due to the generosity and grace of Allah (Exalted is He), that He make this *Shahadatain* a means of remission of past sins. We will quote some *hadith* which supports that and also the possibility of having future sins forgiven.

A DEFENSE AND CLARIFICATION OF THE TARIQA TIJANIYYA AND THE TIJANIS

Do you not consider the combatants of Badr and the Prophet'sssaying? *"It is as if Allah turned to the Companions of Badr and said: 'Do what you will, I have forgiven you!'*

On the authority of Abu Hurayra ﷺ, the Prophet ﷺ said: 'Whoever fasts the month of Ramadan with faith and hope of Divine reward will have his/her previous and future sins forgiven.' and also: 'Whoever prays Laylatul Qadr (The Night of Decree) with faith and hope of Divine reward will have his/her previous and future sins forgiven.'

In the two authentic (*Sahih*) collections of Hadith (Imam al-Bukhari & Imam Muslim), The Prophet ﷺ is recorded as saying: "Whoever coincides his saying 'Ameen' with the Angels saying 'Ameen', will have their previous sins forgiven".[74] Also, "Whoever fasts on the Day of 'Arafat (9th of Dhu'l Hijja) will have the sins of the previous year and the year to come forgiven". The fast on the Day of 'Ashura (10th of Muharram) also erases the sins of the previous year. Also, performing Salatul Jumu'a (the Friday prayer) as the ProphetSsaid: "Whoever makes a perfect ablution (*wudhu*) or takes a full bath (ghusl) on Yawmul Jumu'a, then moves towards the place of prayer and listens to the speech (*khutba*) of the Imam while being silent, and then prays 2 raka'at of Salatul Jumu'a, will have their sins forgiven from one Friday to the next, plus 3 more days." (i.e. Sat./Sun./Mon.).[75]

Ahadith also state that entry into Islam erases all previous sins[76], as well as performing the *Hajj* (major pilgrimage) and *Umrah* (minor pilgrimage) erase the previous sins, (on the condition of course, they are accepted.)[77]

LA ILAHA IL ALLAH IS THE BEST DEED

Narrated by Al-Tabarani in his "Book of Invocations" *(Kitab ad-Du'a)*, On the authority of Abu Dharr ﷺ who said:

> I said, O Messenger of Allah, teach me an action which brings me closer to Paradise and moves me away from the Fire. He said, 'Whenever you commit a sin, follow it with a good action; for a single good deed equals ten sins'. I said, O Messenger of Allah, is saying 'There is no god but Allah' (La ilaha il Allah) among the good deeds? He ﷺ said, 'It is the best of the good deeds!" (Ahsan'l Hasanat)[78]

This hadith is the foundation of the other which says: *"Erase the sinful deed by following it with a good act".*[79] Nevertheless, we know that the sinners will necessarily undergo punishment, according to (other) authentic hadith. But it so happens that this (punishment) occurs to some individuals and not others, by the Favor and Grace of Allah. *"He forgives whom He wills, and punishes whom He wills. And Allah is Ever Oft-Forgiving, Most Merciful."* (48:14).

WHOEVER BEARS WITNESS TO LA ILAHA IL ALLAH ENTERS THE PARADISE

On the authority of Abu Hurayra ﷺ, the Prophet ﷺ said to Abu Dharr al-Ghifari ﷺ,

Announce to the people that whoever bears witness to 'La ilaha il Allah, Muhammadur Rasul Allah' is entitled to the Garden of Paradise. Abu Dharr said, "Even if he is guilty of sexual misconduct and theft?" The Prophet said, "Even if he is guilty of sexual misconduct and theft." He repeated this three times, and on the third occasion he said, "Even if he is guilty of sexual misconduct and theft...in Åite of Abu Dharr's disapproval!"⁸⁰

BEARING WITNESS TO LA ILAHA IL ALLAH IS AN EXPIATION

In a hadith narrated on the authority of Abu Bakr as-Sadiq ؓ who said: "I asked the Messenger Of Allah ﷺ what expiates our sins? He said: 'Bearing witness to "There is no god but Allah!"'"

LA ILAHA IL ALLAH ERASES THE SINS

On the authority of Thabit ؓ, who relates on the authority of Anas ؓ:

> A man came to the Prophet ﷺ and said: 'O Messenger of Allah, there is no sin that I haven't committed!' The Prophet said: 'Do you bear witness there is no god but Allah and I am the Messenger of Allah?' The man said: 'Yes.' Then the Prophet said: 'This (Shahada) takes precedence over that' (those sins).⁸¹

LA ILAHA IL ALLAH IS SALVATION FOR HE WHO BEARS WITNESS

On the authority of Ibn Umar ﷺ, who relates on the authority of Abu Bakr as-Sadiq ﷺ, who said: *"I asked the Messenger of Allah ﷺ, 'How will we escape our current situation?' He said: 'Whoever bears witness there is no god but Allah, who is Alone and without partner and that I am His Messenger, this is how you will attain salvation and safety!'* "[82]

FALSE SWEARING LA ILAHA IL ALLAH REQUIRES EXPIATION

On the authority of Ibn 'Abbas ﷺ, who said:

> Two men came to the Prophets. One of them was seeking a right from his companion. When he was asked to produce evidence and proof of his claim, he said he had none. So, the other man (defendant) swore an oath, 'By Allah, the One besides whom there is no god!, you have no rightful claim against me!' The Prophet ﷺ told (the defendant) that he was lying and told him to give his brother his right and told the man to make expiation (kaffara) for his false swearing by 'La ilaha ila Allah.

LA ILAHA IL ALLAH IS SAFETY FOR THE ONE WHO SAYS IT

Abu Da'ud and An-Nasa'i report al-Miqdad ؓ as saying:

> I asked the Messenger of Allah saying, 'What if an (unbelieving) man strike and cut my hand off and then says: 'There is no god but Allah'-may I kill him?' The Prophet ﷺ said, 'No', two or three times, and then added, '...unless you have become like he was before he said what he said and he has become as you were before you did what you did!'. [83]

LA ILAHA IL ALLAH IS A TREASURE

On the authority of Ibn Hajira (Abdur-Rahman Khawlani Misri), who relates on the authority of Abu Dharr ؓ, that the treasure mentioned by Allah in His book— *(Surah Al-Kahf 18:82)*

> ...As for the wall, it belonged to two orphan boys in the town; and there was under it a treasure belonging to them and their father was a righteous man; and your Lord intended that they should attain their age of full strength and take out their treasure as a mercy from your Lord. And I did them not of my own accord. That is the interpretation of those (things) over which you could not hold patience."—was a golden plate or board *(Lawh)* on which was inscribed: "In the name

of Allah, The Compassionate, The Most Merciful. I am astonished at someone who has certainty in predestination/fate (qadr) who is stressful in this world; I am astonished at someone who remembers the Fire and then laughs; I am astonished at someone who remembers death and then is heedless; There is no god but Allah and Muhammad is the Messenger of Allah ﷺ.

On the authority of al-Mughira ibn Ziyad who relates on the authority of ash-Sha'bi ؓ, who said that Ibn 'Abbas ؓ said: "The treasure that Allah mentioned in His book

> ...and there was under it a treasure belonging to two orphan boys..."(Al-Qur'an 18:82), was a golden plate or board (Lawh) on which was written: "I bear witness there is no god but Allah and Muhammad is the Messenger of Allah; I am astonished at someone who has certainty in predestination/fate (qadr) and stresses and fatigues himself in this world; I am astonished at someone who sees how the affairs of this world constantly fluctuate and change (the vicissitudes of life) and yet can remain tranquil and at peace with it.

LA ILAHA IL ALLAH ON THE EAR OF A FISH

In a report by Abu'l Abbas Muhammad ibn Ya'qub al-Asim, who said he heard al-Hasan ibn Ishaq ibn Yazid al-'Attar say:

> We were traveling from Egypt to (southern) Africa and we had to halt and come to a standstill due to it becoming very windy and we ended up in a place

called "Astarun". There was a child with us named Ayman who had with him a fish-hook and he caught a fish about the size of the span of a hand or smaller. He said it was on the shore. On its right ear was written "There is no god but Allah" and on the left ear it had "Muhammad is the Messenger of Allah". These inscriptions were clearer than engraving on a stone! He said the fish was white and the writing was black, like the writing of ink. We threw the fish back in the water and the people stopped fishing in this part of the sea until we left.

LA ILAHA IL ALLAH ON THE PILLAR OF AL-JANNAT

Reported from 'Ali ibn 'Asim on the authority of Hamid, who reports on the authority of Anas ibn Malik ﷺ, who said the Prophets said:

> When I was taken up to the heavens (Isra' wa'l Mi'raj) and I entered the Garden (al-jannat), I saw on the pillars of Paradise three (3) lines of writing in golden inscription. The first (1st) had: "There is no god but Allah, Muhammad is the Messenger of Allah; The second (2nd) had: "We found what preceded us, we profited from what we ate, we lost what we neglected"; The third (3rd) had: "A sinful Ummah and a forgiving Lord"

It is Allah who inspires us to what is correct and guides us to what is righteous in words and deeds!

Is it acceptable for you to prohibit and ridicule us while we honor you?"
  Or that we protect you and you injure us?

The best of speech is that which is concise and clear (and not long and tedious), and yet gives guidance. It is Allah who guides to His path and surely Allah speaks the truth!

VERSES OF POETRY CONCERNING THE TARIQA TIJANIYYA AND ITS LITANIES

Here I bring forth some beautiful verses of poetry from the unique of his time in knowledge, righteousness, justice and equality. One of the last fair judges. The erudite scholar, Sidi Mahandan Baba al-Deymani ﷺ who gives clear advice concerning this Tariqa and its virtues and merits.

All praise belongs to Allah, The Generous, The Guide
    for guiding us to the easiest of the litanies (Awrad),
Conforming to the pure and natural Deen (of Islam)
    (a way for Allah) to forgive a person and light (his way)
Then prayers of peace and blessings upon the Prophet-the Seal, the Majestic
    who delivered the Revelation as he was ordered,
He who distinguished the special deserving people by giving the Secret and
    revealing the Shari'a (for the common/general people as well as the elite),
And also upon his Family and Companions, the rightly-guided on the path of
    guidance and salvation,
And also upon everyone who follows their path in Ihsan (spiritual perfection),
    like our Shaykh Tijani!
After this, you should know—those near and far, that whosoever is joined to
    this Tariqa is happy and blessed,
Verily, the group/party who neglects and omits has lost, when they deny and

prohibit this Tariqa Tijaniyya!
Prohibiting people from the Tariqa when they desire it, and denying them the
> Awrad (litanies) of the Tariqa,
Is the Awrad anything but the remembrance of Allah?
> To prohibit someone from that is prohibited, O you who prohibit!!
Allah gave the command to increase and make ALOT of dhikr, O you who
> prohibit the remembrance!
And He did not specify a limit or a particular form,
> So nothing about the dhikr could be innovation,
Everything that comes without specification
> is general and open to everyone (common/general people),
They also prohibit the 'Jawharatul Kamal',
> In spite of the clarity of this Deen in its perfection,
The ignorant do not know the comprehensive and general order of sending
> peace and blessings upon the Prophet, using any and every form to send Salat!
The Aqtab (Cardinal Poles) among the Saints never cease, from taking from
> The Imam of the Prophets—after his death—the secret knowledges,
like ash-Shadhili in his taking the "Hizb'l Bahr"!
> Or as-Suyuti shaking hands in Cairo,
with his hands to the pure hands of the Prophet!
> The lineage of our Shaykh al-Tijani,
is related to that of the Messenger in 'Sealing'!
Because of their ignorance of the incomings (waridat) of this wird and in spite of the fact that this wird is found in the text of Al-Qur'an without
any abrogation!
They also prohibit the spreading of the white sheet (al-'izar) out of honor and respect for the attendance of the Prophet. [84]
They also deny the attendance of the Prophet
> at our 'Jawharatul Kamal' because of lack of knowledge,
When surely Abu Bakr as-Siddiq spread (the garment) for the angels!
> They also prohibit & deny audible and group dhikr,

Although both are permissible according to consensus (ijma'a)
   For the consensus has come to pass after the disagreement (ikhtilaf) over it.
So it is permissible today without any disagreement!
   They weigh and estimate the dhikr with the wrong judgment,
   For they do not weigh with the Shari'a!"

There is more to this poem (as it is very lengthy).

FROM THE QASIDA OF AMIR AL-MUMINEEN MUHAMMAD BELLO (D.1837) IN PRAISE OF SHAYKH AHMAD AL-TIJANI

I will now bring some of the poetry of *Amir Al-Mumineen* Muhammad Bello ibn Shaykh 'Uthman ibn Fodi ﷺ, Emir of the Sokoto Caliphate, in praise of his Shaykh, al-*Khatm* Ahmad al-Tijani ﷺ:

Leave from the houses and those who live in them,
   Leave from Salma, Hind and Rubab and ask about their state,
Leave away from remembering them for there is no benefit in it,
   It will not enrich you in anything except anger, grief and stress,
It is empty and destroyed—the place and the people who used to live there,
   Along with those who follow them (in these useless places),
Rather, remember those (righteous Sufis) whom you have met
   in the country, but leave remembering flirting and wooing with women,
(Remember) those who are the highly exalted people—lofty as the heavens,
   Spread and circulate their mention by the grace of Ar-Rahman,
Never lean on anyone besides them, never!
   Never let any barrier or veil come between you and them!
Don't be pleased or satisfied with any good fortune except their good
   fortune, that is, if you desire good and pleasant things,

A DEFENSE AND CLARIFICATION OF THE TARIQA TIJANIYYA AND THE TIJANIS

They are the kings and there are no kings nor kingdom besides them,
  The people of their company obtain all that brings satisfaction,
Don't work or occupy yourself with anything except to be in their number,
  Otherwise, you will be among those drowning in the sea of tyranny,
Jump to follow their steps in submitting to Allah,
  And ask for guidance, success (tawfeeq) and His good pleasure,
Come to where they come and drink what they drink,
  Be present in their gatherings for the love of Ar-Rahman,
Live where they live and go where they go,
  Plant and sow where they plant and sow and be ready for work!
For they are the isthmus' (baraazikh) and none is given but by them,
  They are wonderful Patrons and Guardians! - especially al-Tijani,
We ask Allah for guidance and success by the rank of them,
  And by the rank of their well-known Shaykh...al-Tijani,
By his rank, my Lord, forgive and pardon our sins,
  And save us, our Lord, from the heat of the hellfire,
Pull your servant to the gathering of unveiling
  the screens and cloaks—-by the rank of Shaykh Tijani,
Until the Lights of Divine Majesty rise upon me
  Without (mixing) the caprices of the ego-self or the fate of Shaytan,
So that I won't be (veiled) by the confusion of the Universe,
  from witnessing Your Essence in the Presence of Your Dominion,
My Lord, I ask You by our master, the Chosen—al-Mukhtar
  Peace and blessings upon him for all time,
I ask for Your good pleasure with me and Your forgiveness for the actions
  of my body—-by the rank of Abu'l Abbas al-Tijani,
Remove the veils from my eyes
  Until I witness You in reality and with certainty!,
Establish us in his wird forever,
  And place us in the neighborhood of Your good pleasure,
Cause us to achieve and realize the highest of our aims,
  And complete us in Gnosis ('irfan),

SHAYKH AL-ISLAM AL-HAJJ IBRAHIM NIASSE AL-TIJANI AL-KAOLACKI

Flood us in Holy waters that will cleanse
  Us of all darkness and coverings of dirt,
Forgive us for every act of disobedience,
  And reveal to us the Garden of pleasure,
Mix the love of the Chosen One (al-Mustafa) in my blood,
  So I will be as his Companions at every moment,
Cover my faults with a covering from You, O my support!
  Do not remove the covering, my Lord, by the rank of Tijani,
The Master of Holiness, the Supreme One who is given authority
  From among the companions of Gnosis,
The Ocean of generosity, the Cave of safety,
  The one leaning on (Shaykh Tijani) is given Paradise and salvation from hellfire,
My Master! my Master! You have been given levels
  the like of which cannot be perceived—even by the people of Gnosis,
Your superiority, excellence and virtue have spread on all the horizons,
  The lights of your breast guide us to Ar-Rahman,
If every Noble one has his origin in nobility,
  Then you are the noblest of them all with Ar-Rahman!
You are the highest of them in worth, value, prestige and degrees,
  In acquiring might, honor and virtues and good pleasure!
Your ancestor was the Seal of the Prophets,
  You are the Seal of the Cardinal Poles (Aqtab), O Tijani!
For that is, indeed the true inheritance,
  And none claims it but you, O Tijani!
You are the master of them all,
  By force; willingly or unwillingly, for every obstinate and disgraced,
The light of your face guides all who stand facing it,
  The light of your breast guides the people of Gnosis,
You acquired all the stations of our Master,
  You have all you need of Fayda and Ihsan,
Virtues that hurt the ears of those jealous and envious of you,
  And they burn in the fire of disgrace due to their hatred,
I swear by Allah! the Ocean of Gnosis
  Will never cease to flood and inundate all those who drink!
We ask Allah, by the blessing of your face,
  That He benefit us by you with blessings and good pleasure,

A DEFENSE AND CLARIFICATION OF THE
TARIQA TIJANIYYA AND THE TIJANIS

And that He increase us in Knowledge and Gnosis ('ilm wa'l ma'rifa)
　By the might of your power from the Secrets and Ihsan!

CHAPTER SIX

Praise for the Book al-Bayan wa'l-Tabyin

The erudite scholar, the Gnostic knower of Allah, the Noble and lofty Sidi Ahmad Mahmud ibn Sidi Muhammad al-Kabir al-'Alawi al-Tijani, in commendation and praise for the book "*Al-Bayan wa'l Tabyeen 'an al-Tijaniyya wa'l Tijaniyyin*", says:

> *O you who desire proof of al-Tijani,*
>   *The Qur'an and Ahadith will quench your thirst,*
> *Adhere to the Shaykh (Ibrahim) or look at his writings,*
>   *There you will see Truth with clear proof,*
> *Writings which gather all subjects under one umbrella,*
>   *Along with few words (& not long-winded) giving precise explanation.*

There is more to this poem, but do to its length we have limited it to this intro.

APPENDIX

Tijani Scholars

As an Appendix, we include the summarized biography of Shaykh al-Islam Ibrahim *"Baye"* Niasse ؓ written by his closet disciple and his *Khalifa*, Shaykh Saydii Ali Cisse ؓ (d.1982) as an introduction to *"Kashif al-Ilbas 'an Faydat al-Khatim Abu'l Abbas"* (Removal of the Cloak from the Spiritual Effusion of the Seal of the Saints, Abu'l Abbas al-Tijani) authored by Shaykh Ibrahim ؓ as his major exposition on the science of *Tassawuf* (Sufism) and the *Fayda* of Shaykh *al-Khatm* Ahmad al-Tijani ؓ.

بِسْمِ اللَّهِ الرَّحْمَنِ الرَّحِيمِ

In the Name of Allah the Compassionate the Merciful

O Allah! Send peace and blessings upon the Secret of the Essence *(sirr al-dhat)* and the Interpreter of the Names and the Attributes *(tarjuman al-asma wa's sifat)*, our Master Muhammad, the best of creation and upon his Family and his Companions, the fountains of virtue and bounty. What follows: this is only a (brief) summary and outline of the author's biography:

WHO IS SHAYKH IBRAHIM ?[85]

He is the Shaykh in all his degrees; the tongue of his time and the light of his age *(lisan waqtihi wa nur zamanihi)*; unique in his kind *(nasij wahdihi)*; the focal point of Allah's sight among His creation *(mahal nadhr Allah min khalqhi)*; the open door for all who desire to enter the Presence of His Holiness; unique and peerless in his era in knowledge and *Deen (farid dahrihi fi'l ilm wa deen)*; the Shaykh of his epoch in the spiritual training of the disciples *(tarbiyya't al-muridin)*; the flag and standard of the rightly-guided and the seal of those who have experienced the reality of things

A DEFENSE AND CLARIFICATION OF THE TARIQA TIJANIYYA AND THE TIJANIS

('Alama al-muhtadin wa khatim al-muhaqqiqin) in the 14th century *(hijri)*; the joy and delight of the days and the nights *(bahja't layali wa'l ayam)*; the proof of the renowned Gnostics of Allah *(hujjat'l 'arifin al-a'lam)*; the pinnacle of the Muhammadan Ummah; the helper of the Tariqa Ahmadiyya-Ibrahimiyya-Hanifiyya and the cream of its most exalted men; the sunrise of knowledge and gnosis *(matali'a shamsh'l 'ulum wa'l ma'arif)*; the conjoiner of intellects and intuitions; the impenetrable fortress and exalted cave; the pearl of the crown of the noble *Siddiqin*; the medium by which the priceless necklace of the eminent *Qutbs* is conveyed *(wasita al-'aqd an-nafis min al-Aqtab al-a'lam)*; the bearer of the flags of nobility and dignity among humanity; the restorer of the knowledge of the People *(the Sufis)*—which had been completely separated and broken off—from the beginning of this *Ummah* until now.

He is gifted with a well-pleasing beautiful character and the sacred Muhammadan attributes *(akh al-akhlaq al-hasanat'l mardiyya wa shama'il al-qudsiyya Muhammadiyya)*; Endowed with the highest degree of Divine knowledge and Lordly Beneficence and Gnosis-whereby no eloquent and copious speech can describe, as a bounty and favor from the Generous, the Bestower *(fadlan wa tafdilan min al-Karim al-Wahhab)*; He is without equivalent or comparison in the present as well as the future *('adim an-nadhir wa'l mithal fi'l hal wa'l ma'al)*; He ascended the summit and peak of honor, distinction, purity and perfection by means of the Muhammadan inheritance and the *Ahmadi-Khatimi* spiritual training *(tarbiyya)*; He is the one adorned with the crowns of beautiful jewels; the Owner of hidden signals, tremendous utility and benefit and enlightening communications *(sahib al-isharat al-khafiyya wa'l ifadat al-adhima wa'l 'ibarat al-mafhama)*.

He is our Shaykh and our means of approach to Allah; the unique Lordly Cardinal Pole *(al-Qutb al-fard ar-rabbani)*;

the great Eternal Gnostic *(al-'arif al-kabir as-samdani)*— Shaykh Ibrahim ibn Al-Hajj Abdullahi al-Tijani ibn Sayyid Muhammad ibn Mudamba ibn Bakr ibn Muhammad al-Amin ibn Samba ibn ar-Rida—may Allah be pleased with them all and may He benefit us and our loved ones by him! Ameen!

HIS BIRTH

He was born on Thursday (after *Salatul 'Asr*) in the middle of the month of *Rajab* in the year *1320h* [86]/*1902* in *"Tayba-Niassene"*, a village which was built by his father (may Allah be pleased with him). It should suffice you as proof of its excellence and virtue, as well as the authenticity of its name, which means "Purity & Goodness", due to its being the birthplace of this Honorable Imam—the owner of grand eminence.

HIS UPBRINGING

He grew up under the supervision and care of his father (may Allah be pleased with him)-the possessor of virtue, modesty, righteousness, piety, manliness, propriety, good morals and godliness. He studied The Qur'an, according to the reading *(riwaya)* of Imam Warsh on the authority of Nafi', under his father, until he memorized it completely with a perfect memorization.[87] The signs of nobility had become apparent in him while he was still a youth owing to his readiness and willingness to help and assist. He exerted his effort and sincere undertaking to acquire the official and formal sciences *(al-'ulum ar-rasmiyya)*, their literal texts and its proper understanding, until he reached and achieved the intended goal. He studied them exhaustively and mastered all their disciplines, being the head of the class in a short time. Allah had established him as a mercy for His servants and as a benefit for every town dweller and Bedouin nomad.

His schooling was provided by his father, the owner of firmly established credentials and a well-known reputation, until he received from him, praise is due to Allah, the precious gems of useful lessons and the gifts of the secrets, the invocations and the customary practices *(fara'id al-fawa'id wa silat al-asrar wa'l adhkar wa'l 'awaa'id)*. Then Allah granted him a complete Opening and Victory *(thumma fathaha Allah alayhi fathan tamma)* and bestowed upon him knowledge from His Divine Presence until he became consummate in them. He did not study them under anyone, for he was taught by none but The One Who knows all things *(al-'alim)* by Divine inspiration.

HIS TEACHING HIS STUDENTS THE SCIENCES

He did not cease being diligent and assiduous in acquiring and dispensing beneficial knowledge until many people began coming to him hopeful and in search of such. They received benefit from his school *(madrasa)*, along with the erudite scholars who also received training at his hand, as is witnessed on his behalf by the people of gnosis and knowledge *(ahl al-diraya wa'l 'irfan)*. His blessing thus increased to all the brethren and his rank and degree was exalted above all contemporaries.

HIS ENTERING THE TARIQA

He received the Tariqa Tijaniyya from the unique of his age; the proof of the people of his era; the *Zamzam* of its litanies *(Awrad)* and secrets *(asrar)*; the unifier of its lights *(anwar)* and remembrances *(adhkar)*, his Shaykh and his father, the erudite scholar and helpful model and exemplar, the *Khalifa* of Shaykh Tijani without doubt and the bearer of the flag of his Tariqa in the lands of the West *(bilad al-gharb)*. He is the Shaykh, the Imam, and one of the eminent Saints; the one who joins the Sacred Law *(Shari'a)* with Absolute

Reality *(Haqiqa)*, becoming thereby a guide of the Tariqa, Al-Hajj Abdullahi ibn Sayyid Muhammad (may his Generous Lord not cease to promote him to the *Ahmadi* station). Then after entering the Tariqa, his perfect, upright, serene, well-pleasing and well-pleased soul was filled with ardent yearning *(himma)* and he experienced an increase in his lofty aspiration to the point that had he directed it towards firmly established mountains they would have crumbled instantly! His desire and longing was for harvesting the fruits of Divine and Real Knowledge and tasting the Heavenly Kingdom and the Spiritual Secrets *(al-'ulum al-haqaaniya wa'l adhwaaq al-Malakutiyya wa'l asrar al-Jabarutiyya)*,[88] to such an extent that no one before or after him could even hope to reach!

By Allah! How wonderful are these verses of the moving speaker and erudite scholar, the poet, al-Khandidh, in which he praises this Shaykh (may Allah be pleased with him) in his *"al-Nuniyya"* :

He is the well-known Qutb of the Tariqa Tijaniyya and its crown,
  Its Imam and his good fortunes are its crown.
The owner of the highest degree, beneath which the Gnostics are ranked—
  even if their gnosis ('irfan) is elevated.
By him the status of the Sacred Law (Shari'a) has been enhanced,
  and through him the eminence of Absolute Reality (Haqiqa) has been made prominent.
The evidence and trace of both, but for him, would be extremely faint and unclear among
  humanity, and their pillars and supports would be demolished."

Then he proceeded with the duty of benefiting creation with the knowledge which is bestowed from the Divine Presence and the Lordly intuitive Gnosis *(al-ma'arif ar-rabbaniyya)*, devoting himself to the mission in his nights and his days, his mornings and his evenings.

HIS ASCENDANCY TO THE PEAK AND SUMMIT OF THE SCIENCES

As for the Book and the Sunna, good morals, education, right-guidance, oratorical proficiency, fluency, and eloquence, he feasted on them to such an extent that anyone else was the uninvited guest at his table where they were concerned. This has been witnessed on his behalf by the people of culture and refinement of his time, those nearby and those far away. Whenever he spoke, the articulate and fluent Arabs *(fusaha' al-'arab)* would fall on their knees in front of him, raising their heads and lending him their ears. In his hand was the rein and bridle of the entirety of the traditional and intellectual sciences *(al-'ulum al-'aqliyya wa'l naqliyya)*, so he would decipher their meanings as he willed and extract the pearls from their treasure-troves on the spur of the moment.

As for the Lordly Realities, the Sacred intuitive Gnosis and the Essential spiritual states ,*(al-haqa'iq ar-rabbaniyya wa'l ma'arif al-qudsiyya wa'l ahwal ad-dhatiyya)* he was the carrier of their flag, the key to their doors, their niche, their lamp and their crystal *(mishkatuha wa misbahuha wa zujajuha)*. To him belongs numerous excellent virtues and merits!

HIS EXCELLENT AND GLORIOUS QUALITIES

As for his excellent and superior qualities and the abundance of his benefit for the creation of his Lord, we are frozen, so neither the pen nor the tongue can sufficiently describe them! Indeed, he suckled the breast of excellence, good morals and independent judgment *(ijtihad)*, seeking the pleasure of The Generous and Beneficent Master *(al-mawla al-hanan wa'l manan)*, for the benefit and consolation of the poor and needy indigents, as well as the affluent. So he grew up on the love of that breast-feeding until his reputation soared and his mention became widespread on the horizons. The banners of primacy *(raayaat as-sabaq)* were anchored in his presence without dispute, controversy or dissension. He never ceased to be the giver of gracious favors and bounties and the patron of generous blessings in every moment and time, therefore the fragrance and scent of his bounties, generosity and beneficence were spread everywhere. In short, his excellent and glorious qualities cannot be enumerated, for the records could never completely count his virtue, even if all the pens were used until they broke on the sheets of paper!

THE EXCELLENCE OF HIS POETRY AND PROSE

As for the excellence of his poetry and his prose, his mastery of the skills of rhetoric and expression, and the eloquent use of the pen and the tongue—Sahban and Hassan[89] could not have matched him!

HIS WRITINGS

He is the author of numerous books, reports, beneficial replies and useful letters, in which he resolves the differences in the texts of the Imams, who are reliable sources of guidance. Among his writings are the following:

1. *Kashf al-Ilbas 'an Fayda 't al-Khatm Abu'l Abbas*

   The Removal of the Cloak from the Bountiful Grace of the Seal Abu'l Abbas

2. *Musarat'l Majaami' fi Masa'il al-Jaami'*

   The Charm of the Compositions concerning the Issues of the Compositor

3. *Al-Khamr al-Halal fi Madh Sayyid ar-Rijal*

   The Lawful Wine concerning the Praise of the Master of Men

4. *Taisir al-Wusul ila Hadrat ar-Rasul*

   The Easy Facilitation of Attainment to the Presence of the Messenger

5. *Tayyib al-Anfas fi Mada'ih al-Khatm Abu'l Abbas*

   The Fragrance of the Breaths concerning the Praise of the Seal Abu'l Abbas

6. *Rawd al-Muhhabin fi Madh Sayyid al-'Arifin*

   The Garden of the Lovers concerning the Praise of the Master of the Gnostics

7. *Nur ar-Rabbani fi Madh Sayyid Ahmad al-Tijani*

   The Lordly Light concerning the Praise of Sidi Ahmad al-Tijani

8. *Ruh al-Adab lima hawaa min Hukm wa Adab*

   The Spirit of Good Morals because of what it Contains of Wisdom and Good Morals

9. *Nur al-Basr fi Madh Sayyid al-Bashr*

   The Light of the Eye concerning the Praise of the Master of Mankind

10. *As-Sirr al-Akbar wa Kibrit al-Ahmar*

    The Greatest Secret and the Red Sulfur

11. *Tuhfat al-Atfal fi Haqa'iq al-Af'al*

    The Treasure of the Children concerning the Real Meaning of Verbs in Conjugation

12. *Al-Fayda 't Ahmadi fi'l Mawlid al-Muhammadi*

    The Ahmadi Flood concerning the Birth of Muhammad

13. *Tabsira't al-Anam fi an al-'Ilm huwa al-Imam*

    The Enlightenment of Mankind concerning the fact that Knowledge is the Leader

14. *Ruh al-Hubb fi Madh al-Qutb*

    The Spirit of Love concerning the Praise of the Cardinal Pole

As for the evidence of his virtuous merit, excellence and superiority; the exaltedness of his degree and value; the height of his aspiration and yearning *(rafa'at himmatuhu)*, it should suffice you as proof that Allah made him to be a well and fountain for the spiritual-minded *(manhalan lil waaridin)*, caused him to be a means of hope for the disciples and the seekers *(mu'ilan lil muridin as-saalikin)*, established him as a support for those seeking aid and help, and made him an assistant for the destitute and nourishment for the starving *(thafran lil 'aafina wa qutan lil murmilin)*. Allah also favored him with the *Fayda*, or Spiritual Effusion, which was spoken of by the Hidden Cardinal Pole and the well-known Muhammadan Seal *(Qutb al-Maktum wa'l Khatm al-Muhammadi al-Ma'lum)*-our Shaykh and our support, the father of Bountiful Grace, our master Ahmad ibn Muhammad al-Tijani[90], for it has spread and continued without interruption due to its appearance at the end of the age *(akhir az-zaman)*. At his hand, thousands upon thousands have attained the perfection of *Ma'rifa*, or Divine Gnosis and direct intuitive knowledge *(kamaal al-ma'rifat 'iyaaaniya't shuhudiya)*. Everyday many people would come to him, both whites and blacks, entering our Tariqa Tijaniyya, the essence of Lordly endowments and mystical gifts *(dhat al-manaha ar-rabbaniya wa'l mawahib al-'irfaniya)*, coming from every region of the earth in droves and droves. No single person took this intensely profound litany *(wird al-jasim)* from him without gaining the benefit of Lordly help and support *(madad ar-rabbaniya)*, as well as access to the realms of Gnosis and direct intuitive knowledge *(hulul mawatan al-'irfan)*. Allah has caused the author of the poem quoted above (Al-Khandidh) to gush and flow copiously when he said:

> You have smoothed the hard ground of the Path (tariq) for your disciple,
>   so its rocks are not feared, nor its boulders.
> You are the Imam, its leader and its physician (tabibuha),
>   Its guide, its Luqman, its Sultan.
> To you belong its subjects and its Caesar,
>   Its Anushirwan, its Negus and its Khanqan.[91]

He (may Allah be pleased with him) was the firm and upright carrier of the load and burden of the Prophetic-Muhammadan spiritual training *(tarbiyya an-nabawiyya't Muhammadiyya)* in his time; the holder of the *Ahmadi-Ibrahimi* flag of promotion and advancement; the temple of the secrets, spiritual experiences, lights, spiritual states and stations and the concluding manifestations *(haykal al-asrar wa'l adhwaq wa'l anwar wa'l ahwal wa'l maqamaat wa'l tajaliyaat'l khitmiyya)*. You have evidence of this in the fact that some of the chief sons of our leaders and guides and 'Alawi Shaykhs came to him to join and enter his company, obtain his guidance, cling to his coat-tail and to receive the

Tijani *wird*. Such as: The offspring of our Shaykh and our means of approach to Allah, Shaykh Muhammad al-Hafiz [92], who spread the Tariqa in the lands of the Far West *(Maghrib al-Aqsa)* and the children of his *Khalifa* and son-in-law, Sidi Muhamdi; The children of Shaykh Mawlud Fal; [93] The children of Shaykh Muhammad Fal; and the children of Shaykh Muhammad al-Hanafi.

He cultivated and refined them with an excellent spiritual training *(rabbahum ahsana tarbiyya)*, guided them along the Straight Path and Tariqa, and presented them before their Lord and Master in a perfect state, entering the protection of His Fold, intoxicated by the wine of His Presence, annihilated to their own existence and surviving in perpetuity in Him *(faanina 'an wujudihim baaqina bihi)*. Congratulations and more belong to these exceptional Masters for their holding to the coat-tail of this guiding Shaykh and trainer *(shaykh al-murshid al-murabbi)*, and for not allowing their ancestral relations to the Shaykhs to obstruct them from reaching the Perfected One of the age *(kaamil al-'asr)*. It is ancestral relationship to the Shaykhs that has hindered and impeded many of our contemporaries, as it did others among the people of ancient times. O Allah! remove the veil from us and relieve us of the attachments and blockages just as You have done for those who possess understanding—the people of sincerity and certitude *(dhu'l al-bab ahl tasdiq wa'l yaqin)*. Raise us to the highest station at all times! Grant every success and victory to those who perceive and recognize this Shaykh, keep his company and believe in him, as well as those who see him, submit to him and do not disobey him! Let it be repeatedly spread and broadcast in every region of the earth that he has no equal or peer in the spiritual training *(tarbiyya)* of people and their guidance to the Transcendent Holy and Divine Presence!

Time swore that it would bring us the like of him,
   You have falsified your oath, O Time, so make atonement!

A DEFENSE AND CLARIFICATION OF THE TARIQA TIJANIYYA AND THE TIJANIS

To Allah be attributed the excellence of the one who praised this Shaykh when he said:

A Shaykh who, when he trains, becomes like Ahmad,
  And when he speaks, he is like al-Asma'i [94]

In this same spirit were the following verses composed in his honor by his brother, the meticulous and precise erudite scholar and wonderful poet, the Gnostic knower of Allah *('arif billah)*, Al-Hajj Muhammad *Zaynab* ibn Shaykh Al-Hajj Abdullahi (may Allah be pleased with him):

You must know that the Imam has provided and set up,
  a Spiritual Effusion (Fayda) of that which benefits the servants,
At the hands of the medium of Al-Tijani—
  "Barham"—owner of Divine Lights and Gnosis,
So everyone of you who loves his Lord,
  will find him pleasing as a Shaykh due to his beneficence,
Love of his Lord is evidence of loving him,
  and hatred of Him is also evidence of hating him,
He inherited the secret of our Shaykh Al-Tijani,
  from his ancestor—-the best of Bani 'Adnan,
He revived the Deen after it had become archaic,
  as well as the Sunna of the Chosen One (Al-Mukhtar) of Banu Mudar,
He (re)established the Tariqa of our Shaykh Al-Tijani,
  in our country when the edifice had fallen and collapsed,
He restored the Tariqa of our Shaykh-the firmly established (al-maknun),
  after it had been sold for property and money,
He repaired and rebuilt its structure which had been demolished,
  and had remained barren and empty for a long time like the Cosmos,
Allah raised him up for the benefit of creation,
  and he has deported and banished every destructive and pernicious (rebel) with Truth.

To where he says:

Attach yourself to him if your want and desire is for Him,
  and leave every other work and business altogether,
The chains of transmission (salaasil) of the Shaykhs
  have been abrogated by him along with the snares and the booby-traps,
He has educated and trained the disciples in a perfectly beautiful manner,
  just as our Shaykh Al-Tijani—the giver of bounty and favor,
Verily, by him the eyes of the sleepers have been awakened,
  and by him the hearts of the heedless have been enlightened,
On the Remembrance (Qur'an) and the Sunna has the Imam based
  his actions in every desirable way,
So you must submit to him—O Shaykhs of the time,
  unless you have returned to the most odious and hateful abomination,
Because in secrets (asrar) he is an Ibrahim,[95]
  and in the Tariqa he occupies a grand position,
So we bear witness to his superiority and preeminence,
  and we are his children in respect of The Truth.

To where he says:

In his presence, O disciple (murid), you will be cultivated,
  and he will provide you with that which is beneficial and useful,
He has frequently trained and educated Shaykhs who had previously deviated
  from the path of right guidance, but then were led aright,
Verily, he has come with the authentic spiritual training (tarbiyya Sahiha),
  that he derived from the Sunna—which was explicitly established,
His determination, resolution, zeal and energy (himma) raises the state and condition
  of whoever desires his God—so keep his company if you seek to reach the goal!

THE DESCRIPTION OF HIS
GOOD MORALS AND CHARACTER ﷺ

As for his modesty and the beauty of his relationship with creation with regard to forgiving and pardoning *(safha wa'l 'afwa)*, generosity *(sakha')*, patience *(sabr)*, equality *('adl)*, dignity *(waqaar)*, love *(muhabba)*, trustworthiness *(amana)*, worship *('Ibada)*, loyalty *(wafaa')*, compassion *(shafaqa)*, good character with all of the creation of Allah (The Exalted), as well as his strict adherence to the Sunna of the Best of Creation and the Secret of Wisdom *(istinan bi sunna khair al-bariya wa sirr al-hikma)*, he has no comparison, equal or match! In fact, he is the Pole of the niche of these noble attributes and the Key to their doors *(qutb mihrabuha wa miftah abwabuha)*!

As for the pleasing nature of his looks and the purity of his outward appearance, they need no description, for just as his physical self possessed the Divine Beauty *(al-jamal al-ilahi)*—his inner being likewise realized the perfection of the Essence *(al-kamal ad-dhati)*. May Allah not deprive us of the pleasure and delight of beholding him and sitting with him, both literally and metaphorically! From his light, beauty and the cheerfulness of his face, the full moon derived brilliance in the pitch-black night! In regards to his good relationship with creation and giving everyone and everything its right and due and taking upon himself the character of his Lord—The Creator *(Al-Bari)*, The Generous *(Al-Karim)*, The Bestower *(Al-Mu'ti)*, The Guide *(Al-Hadi)*, The Compassionate *(Ar-Ra'uf)*, The Merciful *(Ar-Rahim)*—he possessed a quality that overwhelms the minds of the intelligent! He (may Allah be pleased with him) was observant of the requirements of the afterlife *(shurut al-akhira)* in dealing with close relatives, as well as strangers and he was a guardian of the rights of friends. He realized the utmost degree in humility *(tadaru'i)*, mildness *(khudu')*, asceticism *(zuhd)*, and true devotion *(taqwa)* to Allah, privately and publicly, and in being detached from everything apart from Him, and having a good opinion of Allah and completely entrusting his affairs to Him—until that was witnessed from him by the common people as well as the elite, the near and the far.

Concerning the love for the Messenger of Allah (may Allah bless him and grant him peace) and his Family *(ahl baytihi)*, Allah (Blessed and Exalted) favored him with a station which had never been attained nor even hoped for *(lam yadraku wa laa yuram)*! This has been mentioned by the wonder of the age *(a'juwba't zaman)* time, the well-known erudite scholar, the *Qadi* Muhammad ibn Abdullah ibn Mustafa Al-'Alawi:

May Allah reward Ibrahim with blessing and goodness for giving benefit
    to the lowliest and the highest in relation to him (al-asl wa'l 'ula),
You see them (ahl bayt) spending time in his house (yuqimuna zaman bi darihi)
    and establishing a dwelling there during the stay,
There they have no fear of thirst or hunger,
    Nor any fear of being made weary or bored by him,
Nor do they fear any humiliation, embarrassment or disdain,
    nor are they afraid of failure and disappointment or anything else!

To where he says:

Among the signs of viceregency (ayat al-khilafa) he bears a sign
    from Allah which is not hidden from those who pay attention,
Upon his face is a luminous and radiant light from Allah,

A DEFENSE AND CLARIFICATION OF THE TARIQA TIJANIYYA AND THE TIJANIS

may Allah refuse to let it be anything but perfect and complete,
The two "Abdullah's" [96] *played their role in his yield and produce,*
for Allah made both of them to be a watering place and caused them to drink,
For in the Spiritual Effusion of Divine Gnosis (Fayda 't 'irfan) and beneficial knowledge, the last resembles the first!

HIS GENEROSITY AND LIBERALITY

As for his generosity and liberality (may Allah be pleased with him), his beneficence and kindness, the overabundance of his many gifts, his Lordly graciousness *(mawaahibuhu ar-rabbaniya)*, his munificence and openhandedness, they are like the ocean and heavy pouring rain, so he leaves Hatim [97] forgotten and void! May the shawls of gratitude for him never cease being stretched out and his achievements never cease being remembered and narrated!

HIS MOVE TO A NEW VILLAGE AND HIS BUILDING THE ZAWIYA OF AHL DHIKR

At the beginning of his affair he lived in his fathers house in Kaolack. When Allah supported him with help from Himself and caused mankind to come to him from various countries and The Exalted gave him what was not given to any of his people before him and the place became constricted for him due to the multitude of followers holding to his coat tails (may Allah bless them), he established a new village on the outside of Kaolack named *"Medina al-Jadid"*, the home of the unique and incomparable Cardinal Pole *(al-Qutb al-farid)*! He built a Zawiya in it and it was founded on the blessed day of Monday, with fourteen days remaining in the Sacred month of *Dhu'l Qa'da* in the year *1349h* (1929). He completed it in an unusually short time for the construction of such a building, but its owner was for Allah and Allah was for him *(kana lillah wa kana Allah lahu)*-no more need be said! It was made inhabitable by the performance of the five daily *Salat*, the reading of the daily *Wazifa* and the remembrance *(dhikr)* of Allah in the hours of the night, at the ends of the day and at all times (in between), silently and aloud. It became known among the people as *"Zawiya Ahl Dhikr"*-the Zawiya of the people of remembrance! This Medina and the Zawiya has been praised in a poem by *Qadi* Muhammad ibn Abdullah ibn Mustafa Al-'Alawi:

The Masjid of Ibrahim is founded upon Taqwa,
and the soil of Medina (Baye) is free of vain talk and sinning,

I have given up the reins, desperately hopeless from adequately describing even one tenth of his perfections, virtues, exploits, achievements and honorable characteristics. Whosoever is acquainted with his pearls, which sparkle and shine, or is aware of the wonderful benefit and utility which assemble in him, his eye will see and recognize the signs of his preeminence and supremacy, and I am of those who bear witness to that!

O Son of Nobility, will you not come close and contemplate what has been narrated to you, for seeing is not like hearing!

HIS RELATION TO HIS FATHER

As for his father (may Allah be pleased with him), he was the proof of Islam; the lamplight of the darkness; the protector of the *Shari'a*; the reviver of this Tariqa Tijaniyya after the disappearance of its lights; the restorer of its structure and its minaret after the collapse and destruction of its foundation; the saintly and pious exemplar; the most precise in judgment; the unifier of what had been divided and separated; the master among the preeminent men of this ideal Tariqa; the greatest Shaykh; the renowned and celebrated Sunni-Sufi, our Shaykh and our master, Al-Hajj Abdullahi ibn Sayyid Muhammad. This Shaykh was the compiler and editor of all the sciences, including the branches and the foundations *(al-furu'u wa'l usul)*, especially the Book

A DEFENSE AND CLARIFICATION OF THE TARIQA TIJANIYYA AND THE TIJANIS

(Qur'an) and the Hadith. I found a book written by the subject of the biography (may Allah be pleased with him), in which he says that his father had taught the commentary and explanation of the Qur'an or *Tafsir*, to the men of Allah more than a hundred times; performed the pilgrimage, or *Hajj*, and visited the Messenger of Allah (may Allah bless him and give him peace); struggled in the cause of Allah with a beautiful and perfect exertion *(jaahidu fillahi husna mujaahida)*, and that he awakened the eyes of the sleepers.

From the saintly blessing and grace *(baraka)* of this honorable master has come to us all goodness, bounty and felicity. May Allah grant him a reward of goodness on our behalf! His virtuous deeds and exploits, his strength in the *Deen*, asceticism, and piety are too much and too many to be counted or enumerated. May Allah give us and all of our children real benefit from him, and may He pour out His blessings upon us and shower us with His fragrant gifts until the Day of Judgment! *Ameen, Ya Rabbil 'Alameen!*

HIS RELATION TO HIS MOTHER

As for his mother (may Allah be pleased with her), she is the precious and treasured pearl; the priceless gem; righteous; ascetic; virtuous; noble; attentive to the Lordly rights *(huquq ar-rubbubiyya)* in her states and her speech. She is devoted to the behavior and conduct prescribed by the Sunna, to righteous deeds and pleasing actions worthy of thanks and praise. She is the essence of abundant blessing and radiant lights; firmly rooted in capability and certainty; holding tight to the strong and durable rope, our Sayyida A'isha bint Sidi Ibrahim. Ever since Allah placed her under the authority of the father of this Shaykh, she never ceased being concerned for and interested in pleasing him, and striving hard to obey him. She never did anything to anger or injure him, or trouble his mind or the minds of the brethren and neighbors. She never raised her voice above his and she used to behave beautifully towards him, rushing to please him and never opposing him in anything whatsoever. Whenever he gave her advice or instruction, she followed and complied. Her relationship with him never ceased being like this until he was transferred from this life to the abode on high, well-pleased with her and thankful and indebted for her efforts. This has been witnessed on her behalf by the elite and the common folk, by loved ones and by enemies alike.

I have been informed by someone whose words I trust and have confidence in, he being the honorable Sayyid and erudite scholar, the greatest Gnostic *('arif billah al-akbar)*, my master friend and companion, the son of Shaykh Al-Hajj Abdullahi, Abu Bakr—that this mother verbally told him about the following experience: In the 1st month of her pregnancy with this Shaykh, one night in a dream she saw herself standing on something and there was a well beneath her. The moon split from the direction of the East and fell upon her and she became afraid for herself and extremely alarmed because of that. The following morning she came to the father of this Shaykh and narrated the story to him. He scolded and rebuked her and told her, *"Stop that! Say nothing about it and keep it concealed. Do not speak to anyone about that again!"*[98] She also informed Abu Bakr that when she had given birth to the child, the father called her and said: *"Do you have any hope for this son of yours?"* She replied, *"I hope for goodness for him, and that he will become noble, virtuous and righteous, if Allah wills."* The father said to her, *"Yes, I also have determination and intention for that, and I know that it will be, if Allah extends his life and gives us the joy of his survival!"*

I have also been informed by someone else whose words I trust and have confidence in— that he heard it direct from the mouth of the father of this Shaykh, speaking about this mother—that she would give birth to a son who would completely and perfectly inherit from him. He said, *"If not,* that will never again be possible for anyone else, because of the women of bygone and previous times, she was their superior."

HER VIRTUES, DEEDS AND MORALS

As for her virtues, morals, excellence, righteousness and her demonstrating good character with every creation of Allah, The Exalted—Divine Words have no end and all the sheets of paper are not sufficient to record them, not for all eternity! All of what we have narrated here is only as much as time has permitted, due to the absence of leisure and free-time. It has been given generously, but in fear of being long-winded and thereby wearisome to the minds and intellects. What we have concealed, in relation to what we have reported, is like a raindrop in relation to the ocean! Our purpose has been to preserve the secrets and to make them unavailable to outsiders.

We ask Allah, The Exalted, imploring Him by the Presences of Prophethood and Sainthood—that He enable us and all of our loved ones and our brethren to derive from this Shaykh a benefit that is both special and universal, enduring for all of eternity. May His fragrant blessings and gifts return to us and may He pour the oceans of His bountiful favor and support upon us! *Ameen, Ya Rabbil 'Alameen!*

The completion of this summary (of the biography of Shaykh Ibrahim) coincided with the forenoon on Wednesday, with eleven days remaining in the sacred month of *Dhu'l Hijja*, in the year 1352 AH (1933), in Medina-Kaolack (may Allah cause it to prosper and may He keep it safe) Ameen! This was written by the *Faqir* in need of Allah, The Exalted; the one hopeful for his Master to grant him the perfection of Attributes and promotion to the degrees of the Noble,

SHAYKH AL-ISLAM AL-HAJJ IBRAHIM
NIASSE AL-TIJANI AL-KAOLACKI

Ali Cisse ibn as-Sayyid al-Hasan ibn 'Andal ibn as-Sayyid Ibrahim (may Allah be pleased with them all).

SHAYKH AL-HAJJ IBRAHIM NIASSE
SHAYKH SIDI ALI CISSE

Endnotes

1. The Prophet ﷺ said, "I was sent to complete the beautiful character traits" (*husna al-khulq*; *Musnad* of Ahmad,Vol.2, 381; and Imam Malik ibn Anas, *al-Muwatta'*, *Husna al-khulq*, 8; al-Bukhari, *Manaqib al-ansar*, 33; Muslim, *Fada'il al-sahabah*,133).

2. In the translation and commentary of Shaykh Ibrahim Niasse's *"Ruhul Adab"* (Spirit of Good Morals) by Shaykh Hassan ibn Ali -Cisse  (d.2008), Published by The African-American Islamic Institute (2001). This book originated in the year 1920 as a 121 verse poem *(qasida)* written in the Arabic language as advice to the "People of Tariqa", the Tijaniyya in particular, and to humanity at large. This is the Shaykh's first known work and it is still widely taught, memorized and studied by disciples of Shaykh Ibrahim ﷺ. The Honorable Shaykh Hasan Cisse ﷺ was the Imam of the Grand Mosque in Medina-Kaolack, Senegal and the spiritual guide of millions of Tijani disciples around the world until his passing in August, 2008. He was the son of Shaykh Ibrahim's closet disciple and his appointed inheritor *(Khalifa)*, Sidi Ali ibn al-Hassan Cisse ﷺ (d.1982), and of Shaykh Ibrahim's first daughter, Fatima Zahra Niasse (may Allah be pleased with her). Shaykh Hassan was designated to lead Shaykh Ibrahim's community of followers by the Shaykh himself, whose last will explicitly appointed him as Imam

following the passing of his father, Sidi Ali Cisse. Shaykh Hassan ؈ was the first to introduce the Tariqa Tijaniyya in the United States in 1976. He studied extensively with his grandfather and was the last person to see him alive.(Wright & Weldon, 2006). He was succeeded by his brother, the erudite scholar and consummate Gnostic, Cheikh Ahmad Tidiane ibn Ali Cisse (b.1955) as the Imam and spiritual guide of the *Fayda Tijaniyya*. Cheikh Tidiane Cisse was the last person to be personally instructed by Shaykh Ibrahim and was also the last person to be with Shaykh Hassan when he transitioned from this life. His father, Sidi Ali Cisse told him *"Whatever Shaykh Ibrahim gave me, I am giving you."* May Allah prolong his life, and allow his knowledge and spiritual station to benefit those in need!

3. There are numerous hadith which address the primordial and prehistoric aspect of the Prophet (may Allah bless him and give him peace), such as: *"I was a Prophet while Adam was still between water and clay, or between the spirit and the body."* (Reported by Tirmidhi, 5/585; Ahmad, 4/66); *"The first thing that God created was my spirit."*; *"But for your sake (O Muhammad), I would not have created the spheres."* (Reported by al-Hakim in *"al-Mustadrak"*); *"Who has seen me, has seen the Truth."* (Reported by al-Bukhari, 3/1080; Muslim, 3/1466). See Annemarie Schimmel, *"And Muhammad is His Messenger: the Veneration of the Prophet in Islamic Piety"* (1985).

In the famous poem by Sidi Muhammad ibn Hasan Al-Busairi ؈ called *"Qasida al-Burda"* (The Poem of the Cloak), speaking on the Prophet's doing without *(zuhd)* and his spiritual reality, it says: *"How could the worldly needs allure him towards this material world? For had it not been for him this world would not have come out of non-existence."* Alluding to the Muhammadan Reality, Allah says in the Qur'an *"The Prophet is closer to the believers than their own selves..."* (33:6) and *"And Allah would not punish them while you (Muhammad) are with them..."* (8:33) and *"Know! that among you there is the Messenger of Allah."* (49:7) and *"Verily, there comes to you a Messenger from yourselves. It grieves him that you should receive any injury or difficulty. He is anxious over you; for the believers he is Ra'uf (full of kindness), Rahim (merciful)."* (9:128) and *"Allah warns you against Himself (to beware of Him) and Allah is Ra'uf (full of kindness) to His slaves."* (3:30) and *"Verily, those who give Bai'ah (pledge) to you (Muhammad), they are giving Bai'ah (pledge) to Allah. The Hand of Allah is over their Hands."* (48:10) and *"You killed them not, but Allah killed them. And you (Muhammad) threw not when you did throw, but Allah threw..."* (8:17) and *"He who obeys the Messenger, has indeed obeyed Allah."* (4:80).

4. Victor Danner, *"The Islamic Tradition".*

5. Shaykh Ahmad Zarruq (d.1493), famous Moroccan scholar of the Shadhiliyya Sufi order who stressed the proper balance between the Sacred Law *(Shari'a)* and Mysticism *(Haqiqa).* He wrote many books on Sufism, including about thirty (30) commentaries on the *"Kitab al-Hikam"* (Book of Aphorisms) of Ibn 'Ata Allah al-Iskandari (may Allah be pleased with them both). He said,

> The relationship of Sufism within the religion is the relationship of the spirit within the body, because it represents spiritual excellence (Ihsan), which Allah's Messenger explained to Gabriel by saying, "Ihsan means that you must worship Allah as if you see Him." Sufism is nothing other than this, since it hinges on the observation (of Allah) after witnessing, or witnessing after observation.

6. Junaid ibn Muhammad Abu'l Qasim al-Khazzaz (d.910) of Baghdad was a famous Sufi Shaykh and the nephew of Shaykh as-Sari as-Saqati. He studied *Shari'a* and associated with Harith al-Muhasibi, who like him, advocated ideas of sobriety in mysticism, the annihilation *(fana')* of the ego-self in Allah and a rigorous kind of Sufism. See Michael Sells, *"Early Islamic Mysticism: Sufi, Qur'an, Mi'raj, Poetic and Theological Writings"* (1996) Paulist Press. Most of the Sufi orders—with the exception of the Tijaniyya (whose *silsilah* goes directly from the Prophet Muhammad to Shaykh Ahmad Tijani)—provide their followers with a chain of transmission *(silsilah)* passing through Imam al-Junaid (may Allah be pleased with him). Imam al-Junaid said, *"All the paths (turuq) are closed except following the footprints of the Messenger of Allah."*

7. In the well known *Hadith Jibril* narrated by Umar ibn al-Khattab and Abu Huraira and reported by al-Bukhari (1/50) and Muslim...*"One day as we were in the company of the Prophet, there*

A DEFENSE AND CLARIFICATION OF THE TARIQA TIJANIYYA AND THE TIJANIS

appeared before us a man having extremely white clothes and black hair..."This hadith goes on to demonstrate that Islam (as a complete way of life, or *Deen*) has three stages, namely: *Islam, Iman, & Ihsan.* The three could also be seen as *Works, Faith & Perfection.* Works being the 5 daily Salat, Fasting the month of Ramadan, paying the Zakat, and performing the Hajj. *Faith* being the ability to trust and to act in terms of what one knows to be true; i.e.—the objects of faith being Allah, the Angels, the Prophets, the Scriptures, the Last Day, and *Qadr,* or predestination. The means whereby these three dimensions may be traversed are: *Shari'a, Tariqa & Haqiqa.* Any understanding of Islam that does not encompass these three (3) stations of the *Deen* can barely be called "understanding" at all. Islam without the third stage or dimension is not perfect and whole Islam. See *"Faith and Practice of Islam: Three Thirteenth Century Sufi Texts"* by William C. Chittick (1992) State University of New York Press.

8. *At-Tariqa Tijaniyya al-Khasa'is wa'l Mimizat* (The Tariqa Tijaniyya: Its Characteristic and Merits) by Imam Shaykh Hassan Ali Cisse (Translated by Dr. Abdullahi Elokene and Zakariya Wright.)

9. According to Shaykh Ibrahim (may Allah be pleased with him), the basic and general meaning of *Taqwa,* or the fearful awareness of God, is demonstrated by uprightness with the obligations and scrupulousness with the prohibitions. The more specific meaning, as understood by the spiritually advanced, is to be perpetually & consciously aware of the intimate Presence of Allah and to never forget Him, even for a moment, as this is due His Majesty and Beauty. These two levels are mentioned in Qur'an when Allah says, speaking to the general/common population of Muslims *(al-'awam):* "So keep your duty to Allah and fear Him as much as you can." (64:16). While addressing the spiritual elite *(al-khawas),* He says, *"Fear Allah as He should be feared."* (3:102). See *"Jawahir ar-Rasail"* (Collection of Letters) by Shaykh Ibrahim (compiled by Shaykh Ahmad Abu'l Fath ibn 'Ali al-Tijani)

10. Shaykh Hassan Ali Cisse, relaying a letter written by Shaykh Ibrahim entitled *"Risala at-Tawba"* (Letter of Repentance), in his paper and speech *"at-Tariqa Tijaniyya al-Khasa'is wa'l Mimizat"* (The Tariqa Tijaniyya: Its Characteristic and Merits)—translated by Dr. Abdullahi Elokene and Sidi Zakariya Wright.

11. Shaykh Tijani had predicted *"A spiritual effusion (Fayda) will come upon my Companions, so people will enter our Spiritual Path (Tariqa) in multitudes. This flood (fayda) will come while the people are in their utmost state of suffering, difficulty and hardship."* Shaykh Ibrahim Niasse announced himself as the bringer of this Fayda *(Sahib al-Fayda)* in 1930—-a time in history which had witnessed the collapse of the Uthmani Caliphate or Ottoman Empire; World War's One and Two; the continued expansion of European colonization and subjugation; a worldwide economic crisis ("Great Depression"); the emergence & rise of Communist, Fascist, Racist, Zionist and Nazi ideologies; as well as the growing popularity of the anti-Sufi *"Wahabi/Salafi"* movement. For more on the *Fayda*, see Shaykh Ibrahim's major work on the subject, *"Kashif al-Ilbas 'an Faydat al-Khatim Abu'l 'Abbas"* (Removal of the Cloak from the Spiritual Effusion of the Seal of the Saints, Abu'l 'Abbas Al-Tijani). Sharikat al-Dawliyya't llTibaa'a (2001) Edited by Shaykh Tijani Ali Cisse (The Chief Imam in Medina-Kaolack, Senegal—may Allah aid and assist him and extend his life). Essentially, the *Fayda 't Tijaniyya* is come to cultivate in the initiated Muslim the direct experience and "tasting" of the Unity, or *Tawhid* of all things in Allah and reveals the 'hidden' truth that all distinctions are illusory. As Allah, The Most High says: *"We will show them Our signs in the universe, and in their own selves, until it becomes manifest to them that He is the Reality! Is it not sufficient with regard to your Lord that He is Witness over all things? Are they in doubt concerning the Meeting with their Lord? Verily, He it is Who is surrounding all things!"* (41:53-54).

12. The year 1150 AH also happens to coincide with the numerical equivalent of the Arabic words *"Mawlid al-Khatm"*—-Birth of the Seal. Each letter of the Arabic alphabet has a numerical value and equivalent, said to contain the "essence" of the letter, so that words or phrases can be affixed a certain number based on the sum of their letters. (Wright & Weldon)

13. *Wali (pl. Awliya)*- Literally, the Friend of Allah. In Islam, *Wilayat*—the condition or state of the *Wali*—refers uniquely to the Gnostic station of a person. The station of the *Wali* is the station of knowledge *(ma'rifa)* of The Real by direct seeing or witnessing, and have thus been marked by the love of Allah. The Prophet said,

A DEFENSE AND CLARIFICATION OF THE TARIQA TIJANIYYA AND THE TIJANIS

When Allah loves a person, He calls Jibril and says: 'I love so-and-so, so love him!' Then Jibril loves him and proclaims it in the heavens saying: 'Verily, Allah loves so-and-so, so love him!' Then the people of the heavens love him and approval and success (al-qabul) on earth is spread out before him...and when He is angry and hates a servant, He calls Jibril and says: 'I hate and I am angry with so-and-so, so you too hate him!' Then Jibril hates him and is angry with him and announces to the peoples of heaven: 'Verily, Allah is angry with so-and-so, so you too be angry wit him!' Therefore they hate him and they are angry with him and hatred and anger (al-bughda') are spread out before him on the earth. (Sahih Muslim; Miskat).

14. Shaykh Tijani would later free two slaves, Mabruka and Mubaraka, and marry them and have two sons with them, Muhammad al-Kabir and Muhammad al-Habib, respectively, thus today the Shaykh's descendants trace their lineage to these sons (may Allah be pleased with them both).

15. *Himma*—Concentrated resolve; zeal; yearning. The creative force of the Gnostic; that faculty which enables the *'arif billah* to link his/her own particular power of creative imagination to the Divine Creative Imagination. It is by the hearts yearning that the goal is reached. All human actions are based upon *himma*, or the will, only the force (of most) is directed onto the illusory canvas of the *Dunya,* or material world. Once the faculty is directed at the non-objective, it reaches its goal, which is not *other* than the Source from which the *himma* has come.

16. Shaykh Abdul-Qadir al-Jilani (d.561AH/1166), the eponymous founder of the *Qadiriyya* Sufi order, the 'first' of the great Tariqas, which radiate throughout the Islamic world. Born near the Caspian Sea, he was the son of the great saint Fatima bint Abdullah al-Sawma'i. After a period of intense intellectual and mystical training Abdul-Qadir received the "Robe of Initiation (*Khirqa*) and was soon recognized by all as both, saint and scholar. As one of the most venerated figures in Sufism, his burial place in Baghdad still attracts numerous visitors from many different countries. His death occurred one year before Shaykh Ibn Arabi

was born, who would later describe him as "a just one *(adl)*, the Qutb of his time and the Imam of the age."—*(Futuhat)*

17. Abu'l Hassan ash-Shadhili (d.1258), originally from Morocco, but died in Egypt. He is the eponym for the Shadhiyya Sufi order found primarily in North Africa. His lineage goes back to Prophet Muhammad through Hassan ibn al-Hasan ibn Ali ibn Abi Talib. He was the *Qutb* of his day and one of the greatest Sufi masters in the history of Islam. He was succeeded by his famous disciple, Sidi Abu'l Abbas al-Mursi (d.1288). For more on his life and teachings, see *"Lata'if al-Minan"* (The Subtle Blessings in the Saintly Lives of Abu'l Abbas al-Mursi and his Master Abu'l Hassan ash-Shadhili)- translated by Nancy Roberts (Fons Vitae).

18. Shaykh Mahmoud al-Kurdi (d.1780), was an Iraqi Kurd by origin but had moved to Cairo at the age of 18 following a dream he had in which Shaykh al-Azhar Muhammad al-Hifni (d.1767)—the famous *Khalwati* Shaykh—was shown to him as his master. He was well known for his saintliness and his frequent visionary experience with Prophet Muhammad (said to be nearly every night) and Khidr, the mystical guide of Moses, as well as past saints such as Ibn al-'Arabi. In one of his meetings with Khidr he received a special prayer called *"Musaba'at al-'ashara"*, which he gave to Shaykh Tijani to perform both morning and evening. Shaykh Ibrahim Niasse mentions this prayer in his book *"Ruhul Adab"* saying, *"... it gives the beginner secret lights and the one who is far along his travels Divine lights..."* For more on al-Kurdi, see *"Abd al-Rahman al-Jarbti's History of Egypt"* by Thomas Phillip & Moshe Perlman (1994) Stuttgart: Franz Steiner Verlag; and *"On the Path of The Prophet: Shaykh Ahmad Tijani and the Tariqa Muhammadiyya"* by Zachary Wright (2005) The African American Islamic Institute.

19. Abu Ishaq Ibrahim ibn Abdul-Qadir ar-Rayyahi (1767-1850), was the Imam of the Zaytuna University and Maliki Shaykh al-Islam of Tunis from 1832 until his death on the 27th of Ramadan 1266AH. Shaykh Ibrahim said about him: *"Were Shaykh Ahmad Tijani to have no other follower but Abu Ishaq Ibrahim ar-Rayyahi, it would suffice us as a proof to also follow him."*

20. Not much is known about this mysterious saint from India, as the *Jawahir al-Ma'ani* remains rather vague as to his history and background. Some have attempted to make a connection

between him and Muhammad Andalib, who was known to have proselytized the tenants of the *Tariqa Muhammadiyya*, which were widely spread across the Muslim world in the 18th century. (Wright, 2005)

21. *Jawahir al-Ma'ani*

22. Shaykh Muhammad ibn Abdul-Karriem as-Samman (d.1189AH/1775) was a member of the Tariqa *Khalwatiyya*, and one of two disciples given full *ijaza* (permission) by Shaykh Mustafa al-Bakri (He was a Syrian Khalwati Shaykh who frequently visited Egypt); the other was Mahmoud al-Kurdi's Shaykh, Muhammad al-Hifni (d.1767). The Tariqa Sammaniyya has spread largely in the Sudan due to the effort of one of as-Samman's leading students, Ahmad at-Tayyib (d.1824). Muhammad Ahmad ibn Sayyid Abdullah (d.1302AH/1885), the Sudanese scholar-warrior who publicly declared himself the "Mahdi" in 1881, was also a member of the Sammaniyya.

23. These could be the same seven names of Allah taught by the *Khawatiyya* to correspond to the seven levels of the soul. The 1st stage, the self commanding to evil *(nafs amara bi'su)*, was passed by affirming the Oneness of Allah—saying *La ilaha il Allah;* The 2nd stage, the self blaming soul *(nafs al-lawwama)*, corresponded to the name *Allah;* the 3rd stage, the inspired self *(nafs al-mulhima)*, linked to the name *Huwa* (He); the 4th stage, the self at peace *(nafs al-mutma'inna)*, arrived at through the name *Al-Haqq* (The Truth); the 5th stage, the self pleased with Allah *(nafs ar-radiyya)*, linked with the name *Al-Hayy* (The Living); the 6th stage, the self which Allah is pleased with *(nafs al-mardiyya)*, connected to the name *Al-Qayyum* (The Self-Subisting); and the 7th stage, the perfected self *(nafs al-kamila)*, corresponding to the name *Al-Qahhar* (The Compeller). Shaykh Tijani added a final stage of the self called "the hidden self" *(nafs al-ikhfa)*, which may correspond to the "secret and greatest name" of Allah given to the Shaykh by the Prophet in a vision, a name only given by the Prophet among his Companions to Imam Ali ibn Abi Talib. This name is said to correspond to the station of Polehood *(Qutbaniyya)*.-Wright. See*"On the Path of the Prophet: Shaykh Ahmad Tijani and the Tariqa Muhammadiyya"* by Zachary Valentine Wright. (2005), Published by The African-American Islamic Institute. This book is undoubtedly one of the

best in-depth sources of information on Shaykh Ahmad Tijani and the Tariqa Tijaniyya in the English language.

24. The author of *"Kitab al-Jami' li al-'Ulum al-Fa'ida min Bihar al-Qutb al-Maktum"* (The Comprehensive Book for the Bountiful Sciences from the seas of the Hidden Pole), completed in 1808.

25. The author of *"Jawahir al-Ma'ani wa Bulugh al-Amani fi Fayd Sidi Abu'l Abbas al-Tijani"* (The Jewels of Meanings and the Attainment of hopes in the Flood of Sidi Abu'l Abbas al-Tijani), completed in 1799

26. As for seeing the Prophet (may Allah bless him and give him peace) after his passing from this world, we mention the authentic hadith reported by al-Bukhari, Muslim and Abu Dawud, on the authority of Abu Huraira (may Allah be pleased with him), Allah's Messenger said: *"The one who sees me in his dreams certainly sees me, because Satan cannot take my shape!"* Or *"He who saw me in a dream, it is as if he saw me during wakefulness."* Similar ahadith have also been reported by at-Tabarani, from the hadith of Malik ibn Abdullah and the hadith of Abu Bakara. Ad-Darimi also reports a similar statement from the hadith of Abu Qatada. Shaykh Jalal ad-Din as-Suyuti (may Allah be pleased with him) said in his book *"Tanwir al-Halak fi Imkan Ru'yat an-Nabi wa'l Malak"* (Shedding Light on the Murky Darkness concerning the Possibility of Seeing the Prophet and the Angels): *"The question has frequently been raised concerning the sighting of the Prophet by the masters of spiritual states. A number of our contemporaries, among those who lack any foothold in knowledge, have gone to extreme lengths in denying that experience, and they have claimed that it is utterly impossible. I have therefore compiled this book devoted to that subject."* Shaykh Ibrahim Niasse (may Allah sanctify his secret) has said, *"Whoever denies that seeing him ﷺ is possible, is (simply) not among those who are seeing him!"* It says in the book *"Fath ar-Rabbani"* by Sidi Ahmad al-Shinqiti, that *"among the graces with which God honored him (Shaykh Ahmad Tijani) was the waking vision of the Prophet continuously and ever, so that it was never absent from him for the twinkling of an eye. And his questioning of the Prophet on everything and asking his counsel in small things and great, and undergoing training at his hands. This is the highest of all graces granted to the people of knowledge."*—

translated in Constance Padwick's *"Muslim Devotions: a study of prayer manuals in common use"* (1961).

27. For a full and complete breakdown of the meaning of this full name of the Sufi order of Shaykh Tijani, see Shaykh Umar Tal al-Futi's *"Kitab Rimah Hizb ar-Rahim 'ala Nuhr Hizb ar-Rajim"* printed in the margin of *"Jawahir al-Ma'ani"*, and long considered one of the foundational sources of doctrine within the Tariqa.

28. *Jawahir al-Ma'ani*

29. *Wird (pl. Awrad)*—A unit of *Dhikr* constructed to contain in it certain patterns of knowledge and self-awakening. They are medicines, and their recitation make them effective in altering the ego-self/form of the disciple or student. Some *Awrad* take hours to perform, while others can be done in a few minutes. In most Sufi orders the *wird* (also called *wird al-lazim*, or "obligatory wird"), is a specific formula that a *murid* (disciple) is expected to pronounce daily. In the Tariqa Tijaniyya, receiving the *wird* from an appointed/qualified *muqaddam* marks entrance into the order. Sidi Muhammad al- Arabi as- Sa'ih says of the Tijani *wird*: *"Entrance into the Tariqa is not valid for anyone without it"*— (*Bughyat al-Mustafid*)

30. *Sahih al-Bukhari*, 8/6307

31. Of all the acts of worship, or *Ibada*, which Allah has commanded the Muslims to perform, none of them have been mentioned in Qur'an as He Himself is doing—with the sole exception of *Salat 'ala Nabi*. If praying upon the Prophet ﷺ is emphasized by the Sufi's, it is because Allah Himself is the First to send His praise onto him! Speaking to the Prophet in his esoteric dimension, Allah says in Surah Qalam: *"And verily, for you (O Ahmad) will be an endless reward. And verily, you (O Ahmad) are on an exalted standard of character."* (68:3-4). As for Allah, The Exalted sending His prayers upon the one who performs *"Salat 'ala Nabi"*, we have evidence of the outcome of this noble deed…being guided and taken out from spiritual darkness into glorious light! *"They are those on whom are the Salawat from their Lord, and they are those who receive His Mercy, and it is they who are the guided ones."* (2:157) and *"He it is Who sends Salat on you, and His angels too, that He may bring you out from darkness into light."* (33:43).

32. Reported by at-Tirmidhi in his *Sunan*, and by Imam al-Baihaqi in his *Sunan*.

33. Cited by az-Zubaidi (the author of *Minhaj al-Khalas*) in his commentary on Imam al-Ghazzali's *"Ihya 'Ulum ad-Din"*

34. *Jawahir al-Ma'ani*

35. Mawlay Sulaiman (d.1823), became Sultan of Morocco in 1792 at the age of twenty six (26). He was well known for his piety and knowledge, as he was given to religious studies and only reluctantly became Sultan, after his brother died. As Sultan he "continued to govern more like an *'alim* (scholar) than like a statesman, referring constantly to the *Shari'a* and the *'ulama* before making any important decision."—*"Morocco in the reign of Mawlay Sulayman"* (London: ME and N.African Studies Press, 1990). He and Shaykh Tijani developed a close relationship, which laid the foundation for his descendants and several later Sultans to embrace the Tariqa Tijaniyya, including the late Sultan Hassan II (d.2000)—see *"On the Path of the Prophet"* (Wright, 2001); also *"Morocco in the reign of Mawlay Sulayman"* by Mohamed el-Mansour (London: ME and N. African Studies Press, 1990)

36. As for these two stations—*Qutb al-Maktum & Khatm al-Wilaya Muhammadiyya* (Hidden Cardinal Pole and Seal of Muhammadan Sainthood)—their reality is far from our ability to fully describe or define here. Shaykh Ibrahim wrote,

> The Shaykh, my master Ahmad al-Tijani (may Allah be pleased with him) is the inheritor of the Messenger of Allah, his successor and his hidden assistance, and his secret to the entirety of existent beings—in the seen and unseen worlds, from sempiternity to time without end. He is distinguished by the attributes of him from whom he has inherited, as a provision from him (may Allah bless him and grant him peace). To the Shaykh belongs preference from his Presence (hadra), and from the Presence of the Bountiful Provider—'That is the bounty of Allah, He gives it to whom He wills, and Allah is the owner of great bounty.' (57:21). He is the confluence (majma') of the saints and their ocean. No saint drinks or

gives to drink except by his ocean, (and this) by the stipulation of his sincerity, as he was told by the master of existence (may Allah bless him and grant him peace).—*Jawaahir ar-Rasa'il, Vol.1*

(See *"Pearls from the Divine Flood:Selected Discourses from Shaykh al-Islam Ibrahim Niasse"* Edited by Zakariya Wright & Yahya Weldon (The African American Islamic Institute (2006). As recorded in *Kitab al-Jami'*, Shaykh Tijani said, *"I am favored by him (the Prophet) with sciences given directly, which none but Allah knows!"* For more on the subject, see *"The Seal of the Saints: Prophethood and Sainthood in the doctrine of Ibn 'Arabi"* by M. Chodkiewicz (Cambridge, 1993); and *"Islamic Sainthood in the Fullness of Time: Ibn Arabi's Book of the Fabulous Gryphon"* by Gerald T. Elmore (Brill, 1999). These are two of the best published works to date in English that I am aware of which deal with the subject with great scholarship and insight and provides vast reference sources.

37. Reported by Ibn Jawzi in his book *al-Mawdu'at*, and cited by Imam adh-Dhahabi in *Mizan al-I'tidal*

38. Abu Abdullah Muhammad ibn Ali (d.318h/905, from the Iranian province of Khurasan, known as "the sage of Tirmidh"(in the Trans-Oxus, near the present-day border between Afghanistan and Kazakhstan). The epithet, *al-Hakim*, suggests that al-Tirmidhi studied philosophy (& medicine), and also that he was a profound Gnostic. The Shaykh also studied astronomy & arithmetic. If not for the extensive quotations in Ibn Arabi's *Futuhat*, al-Tirmidhi's *Khatm al-Awliya'* was, until recently thought to have been lost for over 1000 years.(Published by Dar al-Kitab al-Ilmiyya). al-Sulami wrote in his *K. Tabaqat al-Sufiyya* that al-Tirmidhi was expelled from Tirmidh because of his two books-*Khatm al-Awliya & 'Ilal al-Shari'a*—for which he was accused of teaching that the saints have a seal *(khatm)* even as the prophets do, and that he gave preference to the saints *(faddala'l awliya')*, using as a prooftext the *"hadith al-ghibtah"*-*"Know that Allah has servants who are neither prophets nor martyrs (shuhada'), and whom the prophets and martyrs will envy by reason of their station and their proximity to Allah...these are the Friends of Allah (awliya')."* (Musnad of Ahmad). His disciple, Abu Bakr Muhammad ibn Umar al-Warraq (d.290AH/903), reports

that al-Tirmidhi used to be visited every Sunday by the nomadic immortal, al-Khidr, whom he referred to as his brother.

39. *Futuhat al-Makkiyya*, Vol.3

40. The construction of this sacred *Zawiya* was begun in 1215AH/1800 by order of the Prophet. It still remains the head Zawiya of the Tijani order to this day, where disciples congregate daily for Salat and Dhikr, and other worship.

41. This conference was convened June 28-30, 2007 in Fez under the auspices of His Majesty, Amir al-Mumineen Muhammad VI, King of Morocco (may Allah strengthen him, assist him and may Islam and the Muslims be helped through him).

42. *The Tariqa Tijaniyya: Its Characteristics and Merits* by Imam Shaykh Hassan Ali Cisse (Translated by Dr. Abdullahi Elokene and Zakariya Wright.)

43. Shaykh Ibrahim's *"Ruhul Adab"* (Spirit of Good Morals). Published by The African American Islamic Institute (2001).

44. Shaykh Ibrahim's *"Dawaawin as-Sitt"* (Anthology of Six Poems).

45. According to *"Kitab Ikhraj ash-Shurut lil Tariqa Tijaniyya"* by Shaykh al-Hadi ibn Sidi Mawlud Fal ﷺ, the exoteric *(zahiri)* reason for this arrangement of the obligatory litany *(wird al-lazim)*—i.e. Istighfar, Salat 'ala Nabi, Haillah—is: *"This is the wird by which we seek the purification of the heart, as the purification of the heart is the building & edifice of Allah. The heart is the house of Allah, unless He is prevented from it, or rather, until it is polished and burnished of the dirt and filth of sins and such. So Shaykh Tijani ﷺ begins the wird with "Istighfar" to refine, cultivate and polish the heart of the dirt and filth. Then he follows this with "Salat 'ala Nabi", as it enlightens the heart in order that "La ilaha il Allah" find a place to firmly reside in, as "La ilaha il Allah" does not establish itself except in a heart which is polished and burnished of its sins. This is an exoteric (zahir) secret as to its arrangement."* *"Istighfar"* (*Takhalliyat*—to relinquish, surrender); *"Salat 'ala Nabi"* (*Tahalliyat*—to be beautified, adorned, distinguished); *"La ilaha il Allah"* (*Tajalliyat*— to manifest, or reveal itself; the theophany of Allah).

46. Abu Ishaq Ibrahim ibn Abdul-Qadir ar-Rayyahi (1767-1850), was the Imam of the Zaytuna Mosque & University; a Maliki scholar whose erudition earned him the title of "Shaykh al-Islam" of Tunis in 1832; an equitable and balanced Mufti, and an exceptional poet. He used to teach grammar, prosody, rhetoric and Maliki Jurisprudence (fiqh) at the Zaytuna. He initially took the Shadhili Path in search of the esoteric sciences, but later embraced the Tariqa Tijaniyya after meeting Sidi Ali Harazim (the companion of Shaykh Tijani) in Tunis, while the latter was en route to Mecca to perform the pilgrimage. He eventually met Shaykh Tijani himself while in Fez in 1218 AH/1803 and received training directly at his hands. Shaykh ar-Rayyahi wrote numerous books, khutbas, fatwas, a refutation of the *Wahhabi* doctrine, and several poems in praise of Prophet Muhammad (may Allah bless him and grant him peace) and Shaykh Ahmad Tijani, such as his *"Qasida Siniyya"*: *"The support of creation—Abu'l Abbas, (Ahmad al-Tijani) Whose essence is too exalted to be disclosed on paper. The spirit of existence—the pole, center and support of being, Its secret radiating to men, The symbol of existence, secret of the Truth and its talisman, Its hidden content, its treasure locked away in a safe-box, The reality of being, substance of the secret and its summation, The flood of God—without doubt or objection."*

47. According to Shaykh Hassan Cisse (may Allah be pleased with him), who reported that Sidi Abdullah ibn al-Hajj al-Alawi (may Allah be pleased with him) once said to him: *"What is desired of the Tijani litanies is to smell the fragrance of the Muhammadi Reality (Haqiqa Muhammadiyya), upon it be blessings and peace."* Shaykh Hassan went on to say, *"Such a fragrance leads one to act according to the Qur'an and the Sunna, both of which provide the capacity for security and the foundation of faith."* —-*"At-Tariqa Tijaniyya al-Khasa'is wa'l Mimizaat"* (The Tariqa Tijaniyya: Its Characteristic and Merits) by Imam Shaykh Hassan Ali Cisse (Translated by Dr. Abdullahi Elokene and Zakariya Wright.)

48. Sidi Muhammad al-Bakri as-Siddiq, (1492-1545, may Allah be pleased with him) was the original recipient of the special invocation *"Salat al-Fatihi"*. He was a Cardinal Pole *(Qutb)* and a descendant of the closet and most pious Companion of the Prophet, Abu Bakr as-Siddiq. He received the prayer in a vision, after spending years at the Ka'ba in Mecca fully absorbed in

worship. He saw it being delivered from Heaven on a tablet of light where it could be read on all sides. He said, *"If someone offers it one time and does not enter the Garden, let him arrest its author in the Presence of Allah!"* Shaykh Tijani (may Allah be pleased with him) said, *"For someone who dedicates himself to Allah, there is no act of worship to match it (Salatul Fatihi), none whatsoever! For someone who dedicates himself to Allah, there is no act of dedication that is dearer and more beloved to Him or more splendid in His sight!"* The prayer also has great efficacy in the remission of sins. Shaykh Ibrahim wrote in *"Ruh al-Adab"* (Spirit of Good Morals), *"Persist on (acts of worship) which wipe away sins, the strongest of which is the Salat (al-Fatihi) of this Qutb (Shaykh Tijani)."* This prayer was also called *"al-Yaqutat al-Farida"* (The Unique Pearl) by Shaykh Tijani.

49. Baihaqi has reported a hadith on the authority of Anas ibn Malik (may Allah be pleased with him), who heard the Prophet (may Allah bless him and give him peace) say: *"To remember Allah in congregation with people, after the morning prayer until sunrise, is more preferable to me than the entire world and what it contains. To remember Allah in congregation with people from 'Asr prayer until sunset is more preferable to me than the entire world and what it contains."* Abu Dawud has reported a similar hadith from the Prophet, who said: *"It is more beloved to me to keep company with people who remember their Lord from after morning prayer until sunrise, than to free (from slavery) four sons of Ismail, son of Ibrahim, ancestor of your Prophet. It is more beloved to me to keep company with people who remember their Lord from after 'Asr prayer until sunset, than to free four sons of Ismail."* Also, the Prophet said, *"The angels pray for one of you as long as he remains seated at the end of his ritual prayer, saying: 'O Allah, have mercy upon him; O Allah, forgive him; O Allah be gracious to him', if he does not damage or break his ritual purity."* (Miskat, al-Bukhari, Salat). And the Prophet said, *"Indeed you will see your Lord if you are able not to be kept from the prayers before the sunrise and the sunset, so perform them!"* (*Sahih* al-Bukhari, *Tawhid, Mawaqit*; Sahih Muslim, Vol.1:307; Ibn Majah; Ibn Hanbal)

50. Shaykh Tijani (may Allah be pleased with him) said, *"By Allah, if you were to remember it (Jawharatul Kamal) constantly throughout your life, without any intermission, the Prophet (may*

Allah bless him and grant him peace) would never separate himself from you in the whole course of your life..."—from Shaykh Ibrahim's *"Kashf al-Ilbas"*. This prayer should not be recited in *Wazifa* until after the performance of ablutions with water, not with dust *(tayyamum)*. If water is not available, a Tijani must not read this prayer, but instead should read *Salat al-Fatihi* twenty times—-as the Prophet (may Allah bless him and grant him peace) and the four rightly-guided Caliphs (Abu Bakr as-Sadiq, Umar ibn al-Khattab, Uthman ibn Affan, and Ali ibn Abi Talib) attend the dhikr of the *Wazifa* and remain as long as it is being recited, according to a communication from the Master of Existence—Muhammad (may Allah bless him and grant him peace)—to Shaykh Ahmad Tijani in a wakeful state, not sleeping. As this prayer contains a complex metaphysical description of the Prophet, to better appreciate and understand its meaning I recommend the excellent book by Sidi Muhammad Fatha ibn Muhammad Kannun *"Hal al-Aqfal li qurra Jawharatul Kamal"* (The Locks' Key in Reading "Jawharatul Kamal"), Published by Dar al-Kotob al-Ilmiyah (2007).

51. The Prophet ﷺ said, *"The congregational prayer is better than the individual prayer by twenty-seven degrees."* (*Sahih* al-Bukhari, *Adhan*; an-Nasa'i; Tirmidhi; *Musnad* Ibn Hanbal). Concerning purification with water *(wudhu)*, the Prophet said, *"The prayer of one of you is not accepted unless he performs the ablution."* (*Sahih* al-Bukhari, *Wudhu*; Muslim; Tirmidhi; Ibn Hanbal). See Qur'an 5:6; 4:3

52. The Holy Qur'an is divided into 60 *Hizb* and 30 *Juz* to facilitate its complete reading in a month or two. 2 *Hizb* is approximately ½ of one *Juz*. The Prophet said, *"Everything has a polish and the polish for the heart is the recitation of the Qur'an."* (*Sahih* al-Bukhari, *Jana'iz*; Abu Dawud; an-Nasa'i; Ibn Hanbal)

53. Narrated Abu Huraira ﷺ: The Prophet ﷺ said, *"Allah says, 'I am just as My servant thinks Me to be, and I am with him if he remembers Me. If he remembers Me in himself, I remember him in Myself. If he remembers Me in a group of people, I remember him in a group that is better than them. If he comes one span nearer to Me, I go to one cubit nearer to him; and if he comes one cubit nearer to Me, I go a distance of two outstretched arms nearer to him; and if he comes to Me walking, I go to him running.'"* (Hadith *Qudsi* found

in Tirmidhi, *Zuhd*; *Sahih* al-Bukhari, 9/7405) and narrated Abu Musa, the Prophet said, *"The likeness of the one who remembers his Lord in comparison to the one who does not remember his Lord, is that of the living compared to the dead."* (*Sahih* al-Bukhari, 8/6407) and Allah says, *"Those who believed and whose hearts find rest & tranquility in the remembrance of Allah. Verily, in the remembrance of Allah do hearts find rest & tranquility."* (13:28)

54. Allah says in Surah al-Kahf (The Cave): *"Wealth and children are the adornment of the life of this world, but the perpetual righteous deeds which last are better with your Lord for rewards and better in respect of hope."* (18:46)

55. This book, which was completed in 1799, is the primary source of information and doctrine regarding the Tariqa Tijaniyya. It contains the biography of Shaykh Tijani (may Allah be pleased with him), as well as it gives description of his noble character, vast knowledge and copious miracles. It contains his deeply profound expositions on theological and mystical questions, and it also records his numerous aphorisms and insightful explanations of several hadith and Qur'anic verses. Shaykh Tijani reported that Prophet Muhammad (may Allah bless him and give him peace) ordered its sacred compilation in a daylight/wakeful visionary experience. The Prophet told him, *"This book belongs to me and it is I who have compiled it"*.

56. Sidi Ali Harazim al-Barada (may Allah be pleased with him) first met Shaykh Tijani in Wajda (Oujda), Morocco, while traveling back to Fez (where he was from), after returning from the pilgrimage to Mecca and the visitation *(ziyara)* to Prophet Muhammad in Medina. Endowed with erudition, Divine gnosis and consummate sainthood, Sidi Ali Harazim was known as the "greatest successor" of Shaykh Tijani (although he died before the Shaykh). In a wakeful vision, the Prophet told Shaykh Tijani, *"He is for you what Abu Bakr was for me."* and *"O Ahmad, consult with your greatest servant and your beloved, Harazim, for he is for you what Aaron was for Moses."* He died while in Badr (outside of Medina) after being overcome by love for the Prophet and falling into such a deep spiritual state *(hal)*, that he came to be buried among the martyrs of Badr! Although his grave is no longer distinguishable—like many other tombs in Arabia destroyed in the last two centuries—Shaykh Hassan Cisse

A DEFENSE AND CLARIFICATION OF THE
TARIQA TIJANIYYA AND THE TIJANIS

(may Allah be pleased with him), while visiting Badr some years ago, reports having been indicated the exact spot in a visionary encounter with Sidi Ali Harazim himself!—-(This is according to interviews between Shaykh Hassan Cisse and Sidi Zakariya Wright of Tijani.org/Khalifat al-Akbar Sidi Ali Harazim al-Barada)

57. Sidi Muhammad al-Hafiz ibn al-Mukhtar ibn al-Habib (1759-1830), came from the noble 'Idaw Ali tribe of Mauritania (who are descendants of Muhammad al-Hanifiyya, a son of Ali ibn Abi Talib). He was the leading Muqaddam of the Tariqa Tijaniyya in Mauritania (introducing it to West Africa) after spending about four (4) years in the company of Shaykh Ahmad Tijani in Fez. He was a *Hafiz* of Qur'an (memorizing it at 7 years of age), a leading hadith scholar, jurist, and a consummate Sufi master. Not to be confused with his namesake, Shaykh Muhammad al-Hafiz al-Misri (d.1401AH/ 1980), who was as a renowned hadith scholar in Egypt (Shaykh Hassan Cisse called him the first man of Hadith in his age) and the leading Tijani Shaykh in the country. He wrote several books on the subjects of fiqh and ahadith, as well as works defending the authenticity of Sufism and the Tariqa Tijaniyya, such as *"Ahl al-Haqq: al-'arifuna billah as-Saadat as-Sufiyya"*

58. Allah says in Surah al-Hajj: *"Never did We send a Messenger or a Prophet before you (Muhammad) but when he did recite the Revelation or narrated or spoke, Shaytan (Satan) threw (some falsehood) in it. But Allah abolishes that which Shaytan throws in. Then Allah establishes His Revelations. And Allah is All-Knowing, All-Wise."* (22:52).

59. The subject of the "Seal of the Muhammadan Saints" *(Khatm al-Wilaya Muhamadiyya)* is a very misunderstood doctrine of the Sufis, primarily because only a few saints have obtained its knowledge and have written about it (including al-Hakim at-Tirmidhi, Shaykh Muhyideen Ibn 'Arabi, Shayk Ali ibn Wafa, Shaykh Abdul-Wahhab ash-Sha'rani, Sidi Mukhtar al-ab Kunti, Shaykh Abdur-Rahman as-Suyuti and Muhammad ibn al-Kabir al-Kittani). Ibn 'Arabi wrote in his book *"Anqa Mughrib fi Ma'rifa Khatm al-Awliya wa Shams al-Maghrib"* (The Fabulous Gryphon), that *"...the need for knowledge of these two stations (that of the Seal and the Mahdi) in Man is more imperative (akadu) than that of all the other correspondences of created entities (akwan*

al-hidthan."—-because the gnosis of these two stations and the determining of their correspondence in man make all of the other correspondences in the world superfluous. This spiritual station is the pinnacle of the hidden hierarchy of saints. The defining characteristic of this Seal is his ascendant position of proximity to the Prophet, such that he becomes the intermediary between the spiritual flux from the presence of *Haqiqa Muhammadiyya* to the rest of the saints, both past and future, without them having knowledge of his position.—(Wright, 2005). See Shaykh Ibrahim Niasse's book entitled *"Tanbih al-Adhkiya fi Kawn Shaykh Tijani Khatim al-Awliya"* (Alerting the Intelligent concerning Shaykh Tijani being the Seal of the Saints), which is the most lucid and thorough composition on the subject. The fact that Shaykh Ahmad Tijani (may Allah be pleased with him) is the Seal of Muhammadan Sainthood is well-known and is only denied by those possessing no share of this knowledge and those who harbor jealousy and envy towards Shaykh Tijani, who said, *"No Saint drinks or gives others to drink, except from our ocean—from the origin of the Universe until the blowing of the Trumpet."*

60. Narrated Abu Huraira (may Allah be pleased with him): Allah's Messenger (may Allah bless him and grant him peace) said,

61. *"My likeness or similitude in comparison with the other Prophets before me is that of a man who has built a house nicely and beautifully, except for a place of one brick in a corner. The people used to go round about it and wonder at its beauty, but say: 'Would that this brick be put in its place!' So I am that brick, and I am the Seal of the Prophets."* (*Sahih* al-Bukhari, 4/3535)

62. The Unseen, or *Ghaib*, is one of the two basic worlds— namely, the upper world of spirits and the lower world of bodies, also called the "World of Dominion" or "Celestial Plane" (*'Alam al-Malakut*) and the "Kingdom" or "Realm of the Senses"(*'Alam al-Mulk*). *Mulk*: The Physical, or material world; the world of water and clay. (also called *Nasut*); *Malakut*: The unseen or spiritual plane or level of existence, related to the "World of Images" (*'Alam al-Mithal*) and the highest angels. The "hidden" World, wherein one finds individual souls and subtle psychical realities. Shaykh Ibrahim, following Ibn Arabi's school & teaching, incorporated a descending schema of four planes: *Lahut, Jabarut, Malakut,*

and *Mulk* or *Nasut. Lahut* being the level of the Divine Essence, or Existence, *Jabarut* (The World of Domination) represents the Transcendent and invincible Spiritual world of the Almighty, beyond the psychical realm of the *Malakut.* It is the level of God's Divine command *(amr)* and determination, and *Malakut* the level of the World of Images and the angels—where the order *(amr)* of Allah takes shape before being translated into physical manifestation at the level of *Mulk/Nasut* or human existence.

63. *"When Allah created Adam (peace be upon him), He made him superior to the angels by endowing him with knowledge of the essence of the entire creation. The "names" taught to Adam were Allah's Attributes and Qualities. The descendants of Adam inherit this endowment as a potential capacity, varying in nature from individual to individual. As people's gifts differ, so also do their ranges of accountability to Allah and the particular forms their viceregency must assume. This is so even at the highest levels, as is illustrated in Sura Al-Kahf (18:60-82) by the different roles played by Musa (peace be upon him)—the embodiment of moral righteousness, and Khidr (peace be upon him)—the demonstrator of mystical insight. But the supreme viceregency—universal and comprehensive—was manifested in the Prophet Muhammad (may Allah bless him and grant him peace)."*—-Syed Ali Ashraf (Director General of The Islamic Academy, Cambridge) in his foreword to *"The Secret of Secrets"* written by Shaykh Abdul-Qadir al-Jilani (Translated by Shaykh Tosun Bayrak al-Jerrahi al-Helvati). Imam al-Bukhari (5873), Muslim (2612), and Imam Ahmad (244/2) all report a *Sahih* hadith on the authority of Abu Huraira, which quotes the Prophet saying, *"Allah created Adam in His image and likeness."* Ibn Arabi writes in *"Fusus al-Hikam"* (Bezels of Wisdom): *"In this connection, the Prophet said, 'Whoever knows his (true) self, knows his Lord.', linking together knowledge of God and knowledge of the self. Allah says, "We will show them Our signs on the horizons* (meaning the world outside you), *and in yourselves* (your inner essence), *till it becomes clear to them that He is the Reality."* (41:53). *So since we know Him through ourselves and from ourselves, we attribute to Him all we attribute to ourselves. It is for this reason that the Divine revelations come to us through the mouths of the Interpreters (the prophets), for He describes Himself to us through us. If we witness Him we witness ourselves, and when He sees us He*

looks on Himself." (Translated by Ralph W.J. Austin).

64. *Ziyara*—-Literally means visit or visitation, but in Sufi circles it has the connotative meaning of a pious visit to a scholar or saint *(Wali)* for the sake of learning knowledge or obtaining spiritual blessing. *Ziyara* can also be made to the grave of a righteous Muslim, especially Prophet Muhammad (may Allah bless him and grant him peace), his Companions and the *Awliya* of Allah. Tijani disciples however, are prohibited from making *ziyara* seeking the spiritual support *(madad)* of any non-Tijani saint, but must love, respect and honor them all. Shaykh Hassan Cisse (may Allah be pleased with him) explained this by saying, *"Tariqa Tijaniyya, being the fountain-head of all the tariqas, is their summation and therefore nothing is in any other Tariqa that is not found within the Tijaniyya. Why then will one go out to beg for what he has in excess in his house?"*—in his translation and commentary of Shaykh Ibrahim's *"Ruhul Adab"* (Spirit of Good Morals) Published by The African American Islamic Institute (2001). *"Allah puts forth a similitude: a man belonging to many partners disputing with one another, and a man belonging entirely to one master. Are those two equal in comparison? All praise and thanks are for Allah! But most of them know not."* (39:29)

65. Writing in the *"Kashf al-Ilbas"*, Shaykh Ibrahim (may Allah be pleased with him) mentions a poem which says: *"The speech of the Saints (awliya) I do not understand, because I am me and they are them!"* The Prophet is also reported as saying, *"The entire host of the Prophets have spoken to the people according to their intellects."*

66. By having a beautiful opinion of Allah, the Shaykh is demonstrating the meaning of the *Hadith Qudsi*, where Allah says, *"I am just as My servant thinks Me to be."* Shaykh Ibrahim wrote, *"There are two traits nothing is better than: to think well of Allah and to think well of the servants of Allah. And there are two traits nothing is worse than: to think evil of Allah and to think evil of the servants of Allah."* Allah says in Surah al-Fath: *"...that He may punish the hypocrites, men and women, and also those who ascribe partners with Allah, men and women, who think evil thoughts about Allah—for them is a disgraceful torment and the Anger of Allah is upon them, and He has cursed them and prepared Hell for them—and worst indeed is that destination."* (48:6) and *"...and you did*

think an evil thought and you became a useless people going for destruction." (48:12).

67. *"Jawaab al-Muskit fi'l Radd 'ala man takallam fi Tariqa al-Imam Tijani bi laa Tathabit"* by Sidi Muhammad ibn Ahmad al-Kansusi (d.1877).

68. Abu Abdullah Muhammad ibn Ahmad al-Kansusi (d.1877), a leading Tijani scholar widely respected for his erudite scholarship, even by non-Tijanis, who served as minister for Moulay Sulaīman, Sultan of Morocco. He is the author of the widely circulated book *"al-Jawab al-Muskit fi radd 'ala takallam fi Tariqa al-Imam Tijani bi laa tathabit"*(The Silencing Reply to those who speak about the Tariqa of Imam Tijani without any established facts), Published by The Tijani Zawiya in Tamacin, Algeria (2007).

69. The *Malamatiyya* movement started in Khurasan and the eastern parts of the 'Abbasid Empire during the 10th century, and the earliest recorded mention of the term is found in Abdur-Rahman al-Sulami al-Naysaburi's (d.1021) *"Risalat al-Malamatiyya"*. Their name signifies those who call "blame" on themselves by pretending to commit reprehensible actions. Its most distinguishing characteristics were its abhorrence of hypocrisy in religion and ostentation in piety, as well as its encouragement to pursue "ordinary callings" (Abun-Nasr). The Tijanis are those who are always with Allah and never cease worshipping Him, but who mix with ordinary people and cannot be distinguished from them by any outward sign. Their hearts are so enraptured with Divinity that they find no delight in being superior to others. *Zuhd*, or asceticism, is typically seen as doing-without, but its more true meaning (according Shaykh Al-Hajj Umar Futi) is the "emptiness of the heart" of the desire for worldly things and/or positions, rather than the "emptiness of the hand"—which often is the cause of those desires. Prophet Muhammad (may Allah bless him and grant him peace) said, *"Abu Bakr does not have more merit than you because of the extent of his prayers and fasting, but because of something which dwelt in his breast!"*. In other words, the *MAlamati*, is a type of Sufi who deliberately seeks the disapprobation, or condemnation of common society. For more information on the subject, see *"Stations of the Righteous and the Stumbling of those Aspiring: Two Texts from the Path of Blame"*, in *"Three Early Sufi*

Texts" by Kenneth Honnerkamp (Fons Vitae: 2003)

70. This quotation from Shaykh al-Akbar Muhyideen Ibn 'Arabi is not in the original Arabic text of *"Bayan wa'l Tabyeen"*, but rather was taken from his book *"Futuhat al-Makkiyya"* (The Meccan Revelations), for its relevance to this section. Muhammad ibn Ali ibn Muhammad Ibn al-Arabi al-Ta'i al-Hatimi (1165-1240) was born in Murcia, Andalusia (Spain). *"Perhaps no mystic in the history of the world has delved as deeply into the inner knowledge that informs our being as did Ibn Arabi. Because of the advanced nature of his teachings he has been known for over 800 years as Shaykh al-Akbar, or the Greatest Master."* He is the author of hundreds of books and essays, such as *"Futuhat al-Makkiyya"*; *"Fusus al-Hikam"*; *"Asrar al-Taharah"*; *"Kitab Mishkat al-Anwar"*, and *"Rasa'il Ibn Arabi"*. (Translators Note)

71. Sahih al-Bukhari, Vol.8, Book 73, No.125; Sahih Muslim, Book 1, No.117. Shaykh Ibrahim wrote in *"Kashif al-Ilbas"*: *"If someone is not endowed with comprehensive knowledge of the ultimate extent of the realities (al-Haqa'iq), he is not qualified to level the charge of unbelief (takfir) on the strength of reliable sources. He is therefore like someone who is digging his own grave, or like someone who is setting himself on fire, since he may intend to charge another person with unbelief, but his arrow will pierce his own throat."* Allah says, *"O you who believe! When you go out in the cause of Allah, investigate carefully, and say not to anyone who greets you in peace: 'You are not a believer!"* (4:94)

72. Narrated Abu Ma'bad, the freed slave of Ibn Abbas: *"Ibn Abbas told me, 'In the lifetime of the Prophet it was custom to remember Allah (dhikr) by glorifying, praising and magnifying Allah aloud after the compulsory prayers.' Ibn Abbas further said, 'When I heard the dhikr, I would learn that the obligatory congregational prayer had ended."* (*Sahih* al-Bukhari, 1/841). It is amazing that in our own times most Masajid are almost always eerily quiet & void of the *dhikr* of Allah after Salat or any other time for that matter. Allah says, *"And who is more unjust than those who forbid that Allah's Name be glorified and mentioned much in Allah's mosques and strive for their ruin? It is not fitting that such should enter them (Allah's mosques) except with fear. For them is disgrace in this world, and they will have a great torment in the Hereafter."* (2:114)

73. Narrated Abu Huraira (may Allah be pleased with him): *"Allah's Messenger (may Allah bless him and give him peace) ordered me to guard the Zakat (obligatory charity) revenue of Ramadan. Then somebody came to me and started stealing of the foodstuff. I caught him and said, 'I will take you to Allah's Messenger!' Then Abu Huraira described the whole narration and said: 'That person said (to me), '(Please don't take me to Allah's Messenger and I will tell you a few words by which Allah will benefit you.) When you go to your bed, recite Ayat ul- Kursi (2:255), for then there will be a guard from Allah who will protect you all night long, and Satan will not be able to come near you till dawn.' (When the Prophet (may Allah bless him and give him peace) heard the story) he said (to me), 'He (who came to you at night) told you the truth although he is a liar, and it was Satan.'* (Sahih al-Bukhari, 6/5010 pg.530)

74. Anas ibn Malik narrated the Messenger of Allah as saying: *"I have never ceased to intercede with my Lord, for He will always accept my intercession, unless I say, 'O my Lord, accept my intercession on behalf of someone who says: 'There is no god but Allah'. In that case, Allah will say: 'This is not for you O Muhammad. It is only for Me! By My Might, My Majesty, My Clemency and My Mercy, I shall not put someone who says: 'There is no god but Allah' into the Fire!"*—- Reported by Ibn Abi 'Asim in *Kitab as-Sunna*, by Abu-Na'im, by at-Tirmidhi in his *Sunan*, by Ibn Maja in his *Sunan*, and by Ahmad in his *Musnad*. Uthman ibn Affan narrated that Allah's Messenger said, *"Whoever dies while he knows there is no god but Allah will enter Paradise."* (Sahih Muslim)

75. At the end of the recital of Surah al-Fatiha, or when making supplication, or *du'a*.

76. Reported by Imam Muslim, who also reports a hadith in which the Prophet (may Allah bless him and give him peace) says, *"The five daily prayers, from Friday to Friday, from Ramadan to Ramadan is an expiation for (sins) committed in between them, as long as you abstain from the major sins (al-Kaba'ir)."*

77. Narrated Abu Sa'id al-Khudri (may Allah be pleased with him): *"Allah's Messenger (may Allah bless him and give him peace) said, 'If a person embraces Islam sincerely, then Allah will forgive all his past sins, and after that starts the settlement of accounts...the reward of his good deeds will be ten times to seven hundred times for*

each good deed, and an evil deed will be recorded as it is unless Allah forgives it." (Sahih al-Bukhari, 1/41)

78. Narrated Abu Huraira (may Allah be pleased with him): Allah's Messenger (may Allah bless him and give him peace) said, *"The performance of Umrah is an expiation for the sins committed (between it and the previous one) and the reward of an accepted Hajj is nothing but Paradise!"* (Sahih al-Bukhari, 3/1773)

79. Narrated Abu Umamah: "Allah's Messenger ﷺ said, *"I guarantee a home in Paradise for a person who gives up arguments and disputes even if he is on the truth. I guarantee a home in the middle of Paradise for a person who gives up lying even while joking. And I guarantee a home in the highest part of Paradise for a person who has a high standard of character."* (Abu Dawud, at-Tirmidhi, an-Nasa'i and Ibn Majah)

80. The Prophet said, *"Be aware of Allah wherever you might be, erase the sinful deed by following it with a good act, and behave towards the people with a beautiful character."* (Imam Ahmad, an-Nasa'i, al-Hakim, and al-Baihaqi)

81. Reported by al-Bukhari in his *Sahih* and by Ahmad in his *Musnad*

82. Abu Huraira (may Allah be pleased with him) is reported as having said:

83. *"I said, 'O Messenger of Allah. who will be the most fortunate of all people, through your intercession on the Day of Resurrection?' He replied: 'I had assumed, O Abu Huraira, that no one would be more likely than you to ask me this question, because I have noticed your keen interest in what I have to say. The most fortunate of all people, through my intercession on the Day of Resurrection, will be someone who says: 'There is no god but Allah', sincerely from his heart or his soul.'"* (Reported by Imam al-Bukhari in his *Sahih*)

84. Narrated 'Ubaida (may Allah be pleased with him): The Prophet (may Allah bless him and give him peace), said, *'If anyone testifies that there is no god but Allah, Who has no partners, and that Muhammad is His slave and His Messenger, and that Jesus (peace be upon him) is Allah's slave and His Messenger and His Word which He bestowed on Mary and a Spirit created by Him, and that*

A DEFENSE AND CLARIFICATION OF THE TARIQA TIJANIYYA AND THE TIJANIS

Paradise is the truth, and Hell is the truth...Allah will admit him into Paradise with the deeds which he had done even if those deeds were few.' (Junadah, the subnarrator said: "Ubaida added, 'Such a person can enter Paradise through any of its eight gates he likes!") (*Sahih* al- Bukhari, 4/3435)

85. In other words, unless you become a *kafir* and he becomes a Muslim. This hadith is authentic *(Sahih)* and collected by Imam Muslim and al-Bukhari.

86. As for the spreading of the white sheet *(al-'izar)* during the recital of the daily *Wazifa*: the practice was started by Shaykh Tijani himself. Before the construction of the Masjid/Zawiya, when the Shaykh and his Companions used to sit in the area in front of the Shaykhs house to perform *Wazifa*, he would request a clean white sheet to lay down out of respect for Allah, the Prophet, the four Rightly-Guided Caliphs, and the angels (who attend the Zikr), and the practice is continued by Tijani disciples. It is indeed a good practice to purify, perfume and venerate the place of Zikr, as it is the place of Divine manifestation. There is the hadith narrated by Abu Hurairah in which the Prophet said, *"Allah has some angels who look for those who remember Allah on the roads and paths. And when they find some people remembering Allah, they call each other saying: "Come to the object of your pursuit." He added, "Then the angels encircle them with their wings up to the nearest heaven to us..."* This hadith is somewhat long, but it concludes by having Allah say, *"I make you (angels) witnesses that I have forgiven them."* One of the angels would say, *"There was so-and-so amongst them, and he was not one of them, but had just come for some need."* Allah will say, *"These are those people whose companions will not be reduced to misery."* (Sahih al-Bukhari, 8/6408)

87. The Arabic name "Ibrahim" is derived from Syriac (a form of Aramaic), and is a composite of the two names *"al-Ab"* (Father) and *"ar-Rahim"* (The Merciful).

88. Shaykh Ibrahim was born on 15 *Rajab* 1320h, which corresponds to October 17, 1902. One biography, by Shaykh Muhammad Abdullah ibn as-Sayyid entitled *"Min Akhbar ash-Shaykh Ibrahim"* (2004), has given the year 1318h as the birth date, citing a letter from Shaykh Ibrahim to Shaykh Ali Cisse, in which he writes: *"I think—and Allah is the Best Knower—that the birth*

date is the year 1318 AH...and disagreement concerning this does not harm anything, for this is the pursuit for historians." (Hill,2007). 1320 AH is the equivalent of the phrase "The Birth of the Owner of the Fayda , the Qutb of the people of his time" *(walad sahib al-Fayda qutb ahl asrihi).*

89. According to Sidi Ibrahim Thiam *(Baye 'Zain' Thiam),* Shaykh Ibrahim was not yet seven years old when he had memorized the entire Qur'an. See *"25 Sanat 'ala Rahil Shaykh Ibrahim Niasse Za'im al-Muslimeen fi Gharb Ifriqiya"* (25 Years of the Travels of Shaykh Ibrahim: The Leader of the Muslims of West Africa)—Published by An-Nahar, Cairo (2002).

90. *Malakut-*Heavenly Kingdom. The domain of the World Soul, wherein one finds individual souls and subtle psychical Realities; The "hidden" world. *Jabarut—*The Transcendent Spiritual world beyond the psychical realm of the *Malakut,* it contains angelic and archangelic realities. The "Source" world; Light and Power.

91. Sahban and Hassan were famous for their eloquence and their poetry in the time of the Prophet (May Allah bless him and grant him peace)

92. Shaykh Tijani, 1737-1815 (may Allah be pleased with him) said, *"A Spiritual Effusion (Fayda) will descend on my Companions, so that people will enter our Tariqa in droves. This Fayda will appear when people will be in a state of extreme suffering and difficulty."*

93. *Anushirwan* is the ancient title of the Persian king; *Negus* is the title of the Ethiopian king; *Khanqan* is the title of the Emperor of Chinese Tartary, or the historical region of Central Asia.

94. Sidi Muhammad al-Hafiz ibn al-Mukhtar ibn al-Habib (1759-1830), came from the noble 'Idaw Ali tribe of Mauritania (who are descendants of Muhammad al-Hanifiyya, a son of Ali ibn Abi Talib). He was the leading Muqaddam of the Tariqa Tijaniyya in Mauritania after spending about four (4) years in the company of Shaykh Ahmad Tijani in Fez. He was a *Hafiz* of Qur'an (memorizing it at 7 years of age), a leading hadith scholar, jurist, and a consummate Sufi master.

95. Shaykh Mawlud Fal was the most famous disciple of Muhammad al-Hafiz and was responsible for spreading his

teachings outside of the 'Idaw Ali. He was from the Id-Ayqub tribe of Mauritania, who are famous for their knowledge of jurisprudence (*fiqh*). Sidi Mawlud Fal traveled extensively throughout West Africa, appointing many Muqaddam who spread the Tariqa Tijaniyya in several countries, such as Futa Jallon, Nigeria, Sudan and Senegal.

96. Al-Asma'i was an Arab known for his deep knowledge and eloquence in the time of the Prophet (may Allah bless him and grant him peace).

97. Again, the Arabic name "Ibrahim" is derived from Syriac (a form of Aramaic), and is a composite of the two names *"al- Ab"* (Father) and "ar-Rahim" (The Merciful).

98. He is referring firstly to Shaykh Al-Hajj Abdullahi (the father of Shaykh Ibrahim)-may Allah be pleased with them both; The second is Shaykh Abdullah ibn Al-Hajj Al-'Alawi (the father of Sidi Muhammad Al-Mishry)-may Allah be pleased with them both.

99. Hatim was from the ancient tribe of Tayy of Arabia, and he was well known for his extreme generosity.

100. This story has been alluded to in a poem written by the owner of Lordly signals and Divine realities; the offspring of the Shaykhs; the mine of firmness; the "Yusuf" of the Tariqa Tijaniyya; the poet of the IbRahimi Fayda ; the Shaykh and perfect Wali—Ahmad Mahmud ibn Shaykh Muhammad al-Hafiz al-Alawi ash-Shiniqiti, better known as "Manna Abba" or "Shaykhani" (may Allah be pleased with him): *"We narrate that when Allah wished for him to appear within the womb, His mother saw the moon fall down upon her while she was yet in her home, It was told to her "conceal your vision, for it contains a secret of the position of him" By him the enemies die in their rage and disgrace and humiliation"*

www.ingramcontent.com/pod-product-compliance
Lightning Source LLC
Chambersburg PA
CBHW060401080526
44583CB00012B/416